INVOLVING PUPILS IN PRACTICE

Promoting Partnerships with Pupils with Special Educational Needs

Mike Jelly, Alan Fuller and Richard Byers

David Fulton Publishers
London

David Fulton Publishers Ltd
Ormond House, 26–27 Boswell Street, London WC1N 3JD

Website http://www.fultonbooks.co.uk

First published in Great Britain by David Fulton Publishers 2000

British Library Cataloguing in Publication Data
A catalogue record for this book is available from the British Library

ISBN 1–85346–685–9

Typeset by Textype Typesetters, Cambridge
Printed in Great Britain by The Cromwell Press Ltd, Trowbridge, Wilts.

Contents

Acknowledgements

We acknowledge the contribution of the following people, whose substantial commitment to the 'Involving Pupils' project formed the inspiration for this book, and whose final reports, views and opinions are widely quoted throughout the text.

Ian Boatman (Project Coordinator), Clive Brooks, Mike Snowden, Ros Ward of The Edith Borthwick School;
Nic Maxwell (Project Coordinator), Penny Drayson, Tania Perry of Cedar Hall School;
Jude Ragan (Project Coordinator) of The Hayward School;
Stephen Whitfield (Project Coordinator), David Baker, Corinna Creasey, Don Curtis, Karen West of The Heath School;
Carol Kirk (Project Coordinator), Gill Jackson, Val Scott, Caroline Spencer of Longview Adolescent Unit;
Jude Jelly and Dave Musselwhite (Project Coordinators) of Market Field School;
Steve Sibson (Project Coordinator) of Priory School;
the pupils and students of the above schools, whose ideas, views and opinions have been invaluable.

In addition we would like to acknowledge:

The head teachers, staff, pupils and governors of the above schools who have given their support to the changes brought about during and after the project;
Essex County Council Learning Services Department for supporting the project through provision of LEA staff time and provision of a budget for staff development;
colleagues at the University of Cambridge School of Education for supporting the project in a variety of ways;
other professional colleagues, including Nigel Blagg, Augustine Filson, Mike Lake and Jenny Mosley, who have contributed significantly to the work of the project.

Foreword

Involving Pupils in Practice provides principles and practical examples of the ways in which pupils with a wide range of needs, including emotional and behavioural difficulties and learning difficulties, can become active participants in learning. The Essex special schools and units involved in the project that provided the basis for this book, demonstrate ways in which pupils can become effective managers of their own learning within a context of wider school improvement and developing inclusion. The schools provide feedback from teachers and pupils who report significant improvements in learning, confidence, self-esteem and motivation.

The Government's Green Paper *Excellence for All Children: Meeting Special Educational Needs* gave a commitment to using the Progress File as a means for pupils to identify and record their achievements, set goals and targets and plan their further learning. The recent OFSTED (1999) review *The SEN Code of Practice: Three Years On* noted the most common strengths and weaknesses of Individual Education Plans. It concluded that parental involvement had improved but pupil involvement was still relatively weak. Teachers who were used to discussing progress with pupils, setting and reviewing targets for all pupils and documenting what pupils had done, were more likely to see the Individual Education Plan as part of the normal planning, assessment and recording in the school.

School staff will find excellent examples in this book of ways in which special schools have involved pupils meaningfully in developing their Individual Education Plans and in their Annual Reviews. Pupils were taught the skills that enabled them to become involved. The approaches used to teach them included thinking skills, Circle-Time, and school councils. These approaches led to more assertive and confident pupils who could actively negotiate targets and longer-term provision, including reintegration into mainstream school.

The practice in these schools illustrates the involvement of pupils in teaching and learning within a wider context of raising standards. The project emphasised literacy, communication and numeracy and providing a nationally recognised range of accreditation in Key Stage 4. Recognising the balance between basic skills and personal, social and health education enabled these pupils to be more extensively involved. School councils, far from limiting their activities to making decisions about drinks machines, have transformed the curriculum and teaching methods in these schools. Active involvement in these councils provides students with a real context for citizenship education.

Finally, this book provides the basis for enabling every school to benefit from increasing pupil involvement by demonstrating how, in its own words, **an improving school is one** that listens to the voices of its pupils.

Judy Sebba
Standards and Effectiveness Unit
Department for Education and Employment
May 2000

CHAPTER 1

Introduction

The 'Involving Pupils' project

Introduction

For the purposes of this book, we have understood the notion of involving pupils to encompass a continuum of partnerships, from staff being interested in who pupils are, through to pupils having a substantial say in how an institution moves forward and what goes on in it. Pupil perspectives, we propose, may inform debate on a number of levels across this continuum. In the following examples, we illustrate these possibilities and show how they may contribute to a range of appropriate outcomes for pupils with special educational needs.

In schools where pupils are meaningfully involved, we would expect to see:

- staff and pupils in dialogue about teaching and learning – they discuss, for example, individual targets in individual education plans (IEPs); planned activities and the evaluation of lessons; issues in school development;
- staff actively promoting pupils' capacity to think – for example, staff have dedicated time for teaching thinking skills, promote the transfer of thinking skills across the curriculum and enable pupils to actively reflect upon, and improve their skills for learning;
- pupils putting forward their own ideas – for example, they initiate changes and innovations in classroom activity; instigate discussion about curriculum revision; contribute to aspects of institutional change;
- staff and governors attending to the pupil perspective – they are receptive to and actively encourage pupils' views about, for example, individual preferences in styles of learning; rights and responsibilities in the classroom; the maintenance and improvement of the school environment.

We would argue that pupil involvement will have a number of different outcomes:

- pupils develop self-awareness, self-confidence and self-belief – so that they are able to appraise themselves realistically while having raised expectations

and enhanced aspirations for their futures;
- pupils are more engaged in learning – they are more purposeful and motivated as learners and they therefore become more effective learners;
- pupils become more assertive – so that they can act as effective advocates for themselves and others;
- pupils are seen as and perceive themselves as being members of the learning community – so that later, as adults, they will be enabled to participate as members of an inclusive society.

Nature and scope of the project

This book describes both the process and the outcomes of a project which was introduced by the head teacher of The Edith Borthwick School at a special schools conference held in Essex LEA during February 1995. The focus was on school improvement and effective learning. Participating schools were asked to bid for a range of school improvement projects introduced at the conference. These would be coordinated by head teachers paired with LEA representatives (advisers, inspectors, educational psychologists).

The original project outline presented at the conference can be seen in Figure 1.1.

The original ideas which formed the basis of the 'Involving Pupils' project emerged from work being undertaken at The Edith Borthwick School and were based on the premise that empowering learners with special educational needs through increasing their involvement in the planning, implementation and review of learning programmes would increase their access to the curriculum and the wider skills necessary for independent thought and action.

Senior managers and teachers at The Edith Borthwick School were interested in the balance between *directed learning*, where teachers used didactic, formal approaches to teaching and learning, and *experiential, pupil-focused learning*, where teachers and other supporting adults taught the 'skills' of learning before the 'content' of learning. They were interested in 'teaching children to learn', based on skills such as communication, thinking, listening, choosing, self-organisation, enquiry, prediction, use of information.

In introducing the project at the conference, the head teacher of The Edith Borthwick School asserted that

> too many students within the special school sector, and more widely in the mainstream sector, experience narrow approaches to teaching and learning, where their own preferred learning styles are largely ignored. Disaffection and poor self-esteem result from consistent mismatch between preferred and prescribed styles. Disaffection and poor self-esteem lead to antisocial and negative behaviours, which in turn lead to more challenging behaviours and, ultimately, exclusion.

The project schools would be schools committed to exploring ways in which to empower pupils and students, to give them more control over their own learning,

INVOLVING PUPILS

. . . an action research project
aiming to increase pupil/student autonomy
in learning through empowerment.

Learning – from control to empowerment.

**The project involves the shift of power and
control in learning from the adult, the institution, the
prescriptiveness of the curriculum, to the pupil or
student through:**

- the use of action research models with samples of pupils/students;
- curriculum change and development linking cross-curricular skills to individual education plans and individual action plans;
- the introduction of cognitive skills courses to develop creative thinking and problem-solving skills;
- development of student support and guidance systems;
- pupil/student involvement in planning, assessment and review;
- supportive staff development using nationally and internationally recognised trainers;
- inter-agency collaboration.

Intended Outcomes:

- enhanced provision for disaffected pupils;
- enhanced achievement for sample groups and others;
- more effective pupil support and guidance systems;
- pupils having more input into school decision-making processes;
- pupils having more input into their own learning programmes and reviews;
- improved pupil access to a range of accreditation;
- staff enskilled in student-centred teaching and learning;
- curricular change, incorporation of personal effectiveness, thinking skills programmes into the curriculum;
- production of a research report showing progress, processes and conditions for effective pupil involvement.

Process:

Phase 1:
School project coordinators identified in participating schools. Project targets identified, relating to stages of development, school development plan, staff development plan, curriculum development plan, OFSTED action plan. Research focus and models to be agreed. Pupil/student information gathered and processed. Staff development/training needs identified in relation to project schools' needs.

Phase 2:
Project implementation (half-termly project group meetings, staff development/training events under way).

Phase 3:
Evaluation, analysis and production of final report.

Criteria for participating schools:

- commitment to developing student-centred learning;
- belief in the empowerment of pupils;
- commitment to staff development;
- commitment to whole-school approaches to institutional change;
- commitment to providing increased access to the curriculum for all pupils;
- support from senior managers.

Figure 1.1 The original publicity information for the 'Involving Pupils' project

attitudes and behaviours and to examine the effects of these changes on their schools.

The project sought to use action research techniques in a range of educational settings for pupils/students with special educational needs over a three-year period to observe, record and reflect on the impact of various pupil involvement initiatives.

Schools interested in becoming part of the project prepared and submitted bids to the project leaders, giving details of the school and its priorities, starting points for action, staff to be involved, pupil target groups or individuals, and methods to be used to track change and development. These were considered by the project leaders and schools were informed of the outcomes. Eleven schools made initial bids. Seven schools were successful in their bids and have participated from the start of the project to completion of the final report. Each school was at a different stage of development, had different priorities and covered a wide range of learning difficulties and disabilities.

The participating schools

The seven participating schools are described below. Readers will find contact details for each of the participating schools, and details of the examination and accreditation systems mentioned here, in the separate sections at the end of this book.

Cedar Hall School is a special school for pupils with moderate learning difficulties, age range 5–16. There are 100 pupils on roll and the school is organised into primary and secondary departments. There are 15 qualified teachers and 9 learning support assistants. The school is supported by an occupational therapist, physiotherapist, speech and language therapist and an educational psychologist.

The catchment area is south-east Essex, excluding Southend Unitary Authority.

The school offers the full range of National Curriculum subjects at Key Stage 3 and the following range of accreditation at Key Stage 4:

GCSEs in art and mathematics, Certificates of Achievement in English, mathematics and design and technology, and English Speaking Board, ASDAN Youth Award (Bronze and Silver), St John Ambulance First Aid and Basic Food Hygiene.

The school has links with the Benfleet and Thundersley Inset Cluster, Writtle Agricultural and Horticultural College for Year 10 pupils, South East Essex College of Arts and Technology and South East Essex Sixth Form College for Year 11 link courses.

The Edith Borthwick School is a day special school for children and young people between the ages of 3 and 19 who experience moderate or severe learning difficulties, 154 on roll.

The school has a number of areas of provision:

- an early years provision for pupils identified pre-school with complex or severe learning difficulties;

- an autistic resource provision for pupils from the age of five who are on the autistic continuum and who have moderate learning difficulties;
- provision for pupils/students with moderate learning difficulties aged between 5 and 16;
- provision for pupils with severe learning difficulties and profound and multiple learning difficulties aged between 3 and 14;
- an 'Access' group for students, aged between 14 and 16, with a range of learning difficulties;
- further education provision for students, aged between 16 and 19, with a range of learning difficulties.

The catchment area is mid and north west Essex.

There are 21.5 teachers and 32 learning support assistants. The school is supported by a speech and language therapist who is based on the school site, a physiotherapist and occupational therapist, school doctor, paediatrician, community nurses, educational psychologists, education welfare officer.

The school is organised under a primary/secondary department structure and the curriculum is delivered through:

- a topic and theme plus discrete subject-based approach in Years 1–6;
- a subject-based timetable in Years 7–11, covering all National Curriculum subjects;
- a further education programme for Years 12–14.

All pupils/students follow a curriculum which places a high emphasis on reading, language and communication skills, including information and communication technology, numeracy skills and personal, social and independence skills. Each pupil/student has an individual education plan, drawn up by teachers in consultation with parents, which identifies learning and social targets for that individual. Students within Key Stages 4/5 follow vocationally orientated programmes accredited by lead examining bodies, including GCSE art, Certificates of Achievement in English, mathematics, science and design and technology, RSA, English Speaking Board, AEB, ASDAN Youth Award and RSA Accredited Learning for Life.

The school has well-developed integration links with mainstream schools and colleges in mid and north-west Essex. Students within Key Stages 4/5 have part of their education programmes delivered at the Braintree Tertiary College. Some pupils/students are integrated/reintegrated into mainstream schools on a full-time basis. A group of pupils at Key Stage 3 are fully integrated into Hedingham Secondary School, supported by staff from Edith Borthwick.

The Hayward School is a school for pupils with moderate learning difficulties, aged between 3 and 16, with an autistic resource provision recently opened. Staff have been trained in aspects of autism and the school is attracting pupils on the autistic continuum. The school is in the centre of the county town. Its catchment area covers both city and rural areas in mid Essex.

There are 110 pupils on roll, with five additional pupils in the autism provision, supported by 11 teachers and 12 full-time equivalent teacher assistants. The school is divided into two departments, primary and secondary, each having a head of department. The senior management team comprises head, deputy, heads of department and teacher in charge of the autism provision.

All subjects of the National Curriculum are covered from Key Stage 1 to 3. Accreditation at Key Stage 4 includes GCSE art, Certificates of Achievement, RSA, English Speaking Board, AEB and ASDAN Youth Award.

The school is developing links with mainstream schools in the area.

The personnel involved in the project have changed over the three years due to staff movement from the school. The current coordinator is the head teacher, supported by the senior management team. The whole school, however, has been engaged in a number of initiatives designed to increase pupil involvement and pupil responsibility in their own learning.

The Heath School is a residential and day school for boys aged 11–16 who experience emotional and behavioural difficulties and have statements of special educational needs.

The school is situated on the fringe of Colchester in north-east Essex. The provision serves all of Essex.

The maximum number on role at any one time is 45. There are ten full-time teaching staff and one learning support assistant, responsible for meeting the requirements of the National Curriculum, and the same number of care staff.

The school follows a timetable as closely as possible to those adopted by mainstream schools. All National Curriculum subjects are studied at Key Stage 3. English, mathematics, science, design and technology, French, art and humanities are offered at Key Stage 4 and accredited through GCSE, Certificates of Achievement or ASDAN Youth Award.

Reintegration to mainstream education is a key feature of the work of the school. Links exist with Stanway School (secondary mainstream) for initial reintegration, with mainstream schools in pupils' home localities and with Colchester Institute of Further and Higher Education (Year 11).

Longview Unit is an adolescent psychiatric unit where young people and their families who are experiencing a range of acute, severe and/or chronic mental health difficulties may obtain specialised assessment and treatment. There is a maximum of 12 pupils (aged between 11 and 16) on roll at any one time. A flexible service is offered, in partnership with statutory and voluntary agencies where appropriate. The aim is to help people take responsibility for their own well-being, recognise their inner strengths and resources and thereby make positive changes in their lives.

The Unit is part of the North Essex Mental Health Trust and is mainly funded by the North and South Essex Health Authorities. Within the multi-disciplinary team there is a social work element funded by Social Services and an educational element funded by the local education authority. A team of nurses, many with specialist post-basic training, an occupational therapist, sessional input from art therapists, a consultant psychiatrist, a specialist registrar and a junior registrar on a rotational basis, are all funded by Health.

The Unit is the only one of its kind in Essex and as such covers the whole of the county as well as taking some referrals from out-county. The young people are referred for reasons relating to their health needs and a wide range of diagnostic groups are represented on the Unit's caseload. These include eating disorders, obsessive-compulsive disorders, mood disorders with or without self harm, presentations associated with sexual, physical and emotional abuse, somatisation disorders and acute psychosis. The average length of stay is six months. Some young people may be detained under the Mental Health Act, although there is no facility for secure accommodation at the unit.

The Unit only takes referrals from Child and Family Consultation Service teams. It is expected that some support will have already been provided within the community but that a more intensive, short-term intervention is required before the young person and his or her family return to the community interventions. Young people will not necessarily be on the Essex Stages of Assessment and are rarely pupils with a statement of special educational needs. However, most will have been experiencing educational difficulties.

The therapeutic programme is designed in such a way that each young person can move between education and nursing strands, depending upon individual need, mental state and capacity at any moment in time. Multi-disciplinary programmes of care are individually negotiated and planned, and are reviewed with the young people and their families on a regular basis. The education programme is viewed as one more opportunity for therapeutic change within the overall Unit experience and staff are committed to the principles of multi-disciplinary working. Accreditation is offered through individual records of achievement and internal certification, and through RSA, AEB and ASDAN Youth Award schemes.

The teaching team consists of 3.4 teaching staff who are experienced in dealing with a mixed-sex group of psychiatrically ill and psychologically disturbed young people. General objectives include commitments to assist rehabilitation and to maintain continuity between the mainstream school and the Unit. Staff are fully involved in planning admissions, assessments (including liaison with the young person's local school) and in establishing and managing reintegration programmes with mainstream schools.

Market Field School is a special school for pupils/students with moderate learning difficulties, 103 mixed pupils/students aged 3–16. Pupils experience a wide range of learning difficulties including emotional and behavioural difficulties, a range of medical conditions and syndromes, sensory impairment, physical disabilities, complex learning difficulties and severe communication disorders. All students have a statement of special educational needs and none are disapplied from the National Curriculum. Changes in intake have resulted in a significant proportion of pupils with severe communication difficulties at Key Stages 1 and 2, being weighted towards the development of language and communication skills. The catchment area is north-east Essex.

There are 13 full-time equivalent teachers, 16 learning support assistants plus deputy and head teacher. The school is supported by a speech and language therapist and a physiotherapist.

The school is organised into primary and secondary departments, with specialist provision for autism at Key Stage 1 to 3. All National Curriculum subjects are offered at Key Stage 1 to 3. The secondary department runs a subject-based curriculum. At Key Stage 4 students can study GCSE art and drama, Certificate of Achievement courses in basic literacy, science, information and communication technology, religious education and design and technology. In Year 11 students link with the Colchester Institute of Further and Higher Education.

The school has developed integration and curricular links with Colchester Institute of Further Education, Otley College, Colne Community School, the Colne Cluster, Thomas Lord Audley School, The Gilberd and Sir Charles Lucas schools.

Priory School is a day school for 7–16-year-old pupils who experience emotional and behavioural difficulties and have statements of special educational needs. There are 46 pupils on roll, mixed, taught by nine qualified teachers and six learning support assistants. The school is organised into primary and secondary departments. The full range of National Curriculum subjects are offered at Key Stage 2 and Key Stage 3. At Key Stage 4, GCSE courses are offered in English, mathematics, science and art. Other external accreditation includes AEB numeracy and literacy, Certificates of Achievement in English, mathematics and science, and ICAA/Edexcel Information Technology Certificates of Competence.

Emphasis is placed on the development of self-esteem through the whole curriculum experience, and individual education plans form the foundation of the educational programmes offered.

The school has links with South East Essex College of Arts and Technology, South East Essex Sixth Form College and Prospect.

The catchment area includes Essex, Southend and Thurrock Unitary Authorities.

Processes and methods – facilitation

Once these seven schools had expressed their commitment to the idea of developing pupil involvement in practice, two project leaders were identified by the Local Education Authority to coordinate the work of the project. It had been decided prior to the initial conference that there would be two project leaders, one head teacher and one LEA representative, for each project. Mike Jelly, head teacher of The Edith Borthwick School, who prepared the original proposal became the first project leader; Alan Fuller, a senior educational psychologist for Essex, was invited to become the second. Alan had been involved with several initiatives focusing on children's rights and self-advocacy. His skills and knowledge would benefit the work of the project. Participating schools were asked to identify a school coordinator who would prepare an initial paper which identified the focus and starting point for their school. The range of focus points, which were negotiated with staff, endorsed by head teachers and agreed with the project leaders, are listed below:

- pupil involvement in individual education plans;
- pupil involvement in tracking targets and self-assessment;
- pupil involvement in the annual review process;
- the development of thinking skills programmes and materials;
- the review of curriculum to better match pupil/student needs;
- the review of teaching and learning styles and strategies;
- the development of independent learning and study skills;
- a focus on raising pupil self-esteem;
- the use of circle-time techniques to help pupils/students solve problems and find solutions cooperatively;
- the development of student/school councils to give pupils/students a legitimate forum for influencing policy and practice.

These were shared at an initial conference where school coordinators presented their plans to each other, became familiar with each other's schools and their contexts and agreed ways in which they would network. These included:

- project coordinators from the seven participating schools meeting half-termly for twilight update sessions;
- school staff attending a range of training days, conferences/workshops organised to support their work in schools, including circle-time, thinking skills, cross-curricular skills, research methods, evaluation;
- staff from participating schools networking to share resources, plan together, visit each other's schools, provide advice and support, attend training sessions.

Processes and methods – implementation

The project was implemented and developed within the seven participating schools under the direction of the school coordinator. It is interesting to note that the role of the coordinator varied across the schools, from classroom teacher to middle manager, senior manager, deputy or head teacher.

Where classroom teachers were coordinators, the support of senior managers was vital. Key senior managers were identified in each of these schools to enable the work of the project to be supported and communicated at a whole-school level.

In some schools, communication of progress was maintained regularly through staff meetings and information bulletins. In others, the work emerged and grew in a much more evolutionary way. Significant impact was sometimes made despite a low profile across a whole school.

Project schools were funded initially for a two-year period. An allocation from the Standards Fund was apportioned by Essex LEA through the project leaders. This largely met no more than staff cover for courses, visiting other schools, expenses for meetings and documenting the project. Some schools used funds to buy in trainers, offsetting costs by inviting other schools to buy in to the training sessions. Some schools used funding to buy materials and resources to support thinking skills or circle-time activities. At the end of the second year the project schools were given an opportunity to share their developing practice with colleagues from other schools in Essex. Following this conference, it became clear that significant work which had taken place warranted further development, systematic evaluation and wider dissemination.

The two project leaders invited Richard Byers, a colleague from the University of Cambridge School of Education, to join the project in order to support the processes of evaluation and interpretation. Essex LEA agreed to fund a third year to support this evaluation process and to enable schools to provide final reports of their work. The project leaders visited participating schools during this phase of the project in order to discuss progress with coordinators and in some cases provide feedback following observations and interviews with pupils or other members of staff. Project coordinators met in order to discuss and clarify data-gathering methods, such as the use of video recording as a support for observation techniques and approaches to interviews as a means of taking participants' perceptions into account. At this stage, colleagues also discussed evaluation and the options for disseminating project outcomes through a further conference, an interactive website, and publication.

It is important, at this stage, to note that nationally and internationally recognised trainers and professionals made a significant contribution to the work of the project. Jenny Mosley, whose work on circle-time, behaviour and self-esteem is well known, led a valuable day with representatives from all participating schools. Similarly, Mike Lake (co-author of *Top Ten Thinking Tactics*) led a day on thinking skills and their cross-curricular application. Augustine Filson, an associate of the Sankofa Institute, London, was invited by Longview Unit to work with all interested project schools, giving a clear overview of the philosophy, processes and uses of Feuerstein's *Instrumental Enrichment*. Similarly, Nigel Blagg (co-author of *Somerset Thinking Skills*) led a session on his materials and their application. The contribution of these leading figures challenged, stimulated and precipitated new approaches to working with pupils and students as well as enskilling individuals and helping them to examine and reflect upon their own beliefs, prejudices and practice.

The work in most schools has been ongoing since the end of the third year of the project. The book will illustrate, particularly in the evaluation section, how the processes used in the project have become embedded in the practice of schools. The schools still meet informally from time to time in order to update each other on progress. This has been a very powerful experience and has given project coordinators the opportunity to celebrate successes both in their own and others' schools.

Documentation

School coordinators were required to provide regular written updates of the work in their schools. These formed the basis for evaluation and review of progress. They also enabled schools to track each other's development and offered opportunities for cross-fertilisation of ideas and practices. Most schools found that, during the life of the project, the focus shifted and moved as the work embedded into the school. In some schools the project work formed part of the school development plan. In all schools the work informed and impacted upon curriculum planning and development.

At the end of the project, although work on pupil involvement was ongoing in all the project schools, each school provided a final report on progress to date. These final reports drew on a number of sources, including:

- interim project reports;
- videos and transcripts of pupils/students and staff in teaching and learning situations;
- questionnaires administered to pupils/students, staff and others;
- data derived from tracking individual or group progress, IEP targets achieved, pupil/student opinion, self-assessment records, annual review records;
- rates of increased integration with mainstream provision;
- focused interviews with pupils/students;
- focused interviews with staff;
- monitoring of teaching;
- records of group discussions, staff meetings, school council meetings;
- OFSTED reports where appropriate.

Members of the project agreed to write these final reports in a consistent format which is largely reflected in the structure of this book.

Processes and methods – evaluation and interpretation

While participating schools collated their final reports, the two project leaders, together with the representative of the University of Cambridge School of Education, negotiated a process whereby the project outcomes could be published and took on roles as the authors of this book. The project materials were synthesised and emerging themes identified. In an ongoing dialogue with the project's practitioners, these themes were fed back to project coordinators for comment and a focus group discussion took place in order to gather reflective comment and information about development since the project officially came to an end. The three authors of this book have used all available project outcomes and materials in putting together the current text. The final reports from the participating schools, for example, form the basis of the central section of this book, which describes the practice. In addition, three major themes have emerged from the work of participating schools:

- pupil empowerment and enhanced self-esteem;
- impact on school ethos and culture;
- promoting inclusion.

These themes are elaborated in the following section and developed throughout this book.

Pupil empowerment and enhanced self-esteem

Why self-esteem matters

The link between self-esteem and learning is well established. Teachers have long been aware that achievements at school can be influenced, both positively and negatively, by how pupils feel about themselves. Writing over a decade ago Lawrence (1987) identified a large body of research that demonstrated a positive correlation between self-esteem and achievement. Some of the strongest evidence came from studies showing that students identified as having special educational needs experienced lower self-esteem than their peers.

It is important to clarify what is meant by self-esteem given the different meanings often associated with the term. Lawrence, for example, defines self-esteem as an individual's evaluation of the discrepancy between their perception of themselves (self-image) and the image of how they would like to be (ideal self). It is to be expected that there is a discrepancy between the two as even the most successful learners strive for higher levels of achievement. However, the key issue is how an individual feels about this difference. For example, where pupils who are lower attaining have reduced self-esteem they not only view the gap between their achievement and that of their peers as large but they are worried or distressed by this. It is clearly not inevitable that pupils with special educational needs will experience low self-esteem and teachers, family members and peers contribute significantly to the development of these feelings. The actions of key individuals can serve to reinforce negative feelings of failure and contribute to low self-esteem among pupils with special educational needs. However, there is a great deal schools can do to create a climate that fosters positive feelings of self, regardless of perceived difficulties. In this book there are examples of schools actively involving pupils in the learning process, teaching them the skills to take greater control of their own learning and giving them a say in decisions about school changes. It is argued here that empowering pupils to participate more fully in the life of their schools brings about enhanced self-esteem and enables pupils to become more successful learners.

Among the educational trends of the late 1990s there has been a paradoxical growth of interest in empowering individual learners alongside an attainment-driven agenda that seeks wide-scale achievement of nationally set targets. Despite an apparent conflict between these developments their compatibility arises from the realisation that challenging learning targets can only be met if individual needs are addressed. Teaching that fails to take into account factors that enhance or inhibit individual learning is unlikely to result in sustained achievement for the majority of pupils. In looking for ways to raise standards and improve the effectiveness of teaching there is a need to incorporate up-to-date knowledge about the learning process. For example, from the field of cognitive psychology we learn about the importance of pupils actively processing information rather than being passive receivers of knowledge and the need to develop meta-cognitive skills that underpin their learning. Enabling pupils to reflect on their strengths and difficulties and participate in planning learning activities helps to stimulate awareness of how they learn. Actively involving pupils in these ways has a positive impact both on their motivation to learn and their development of effective learning strategies.

Active participation enhances learning

Support for the view that effective teaching addresses individual needs and encourages active participation of learners is provided by a number of research studies since the 1970s. In a review of research into school effectiveness, commissioned by OFSTED, Sammons et al. (1995) identified 11 key characteristics of effective schools. It is significant that one of the factors they found to correlate with school effectiveness was an emphasis on 'pupil rights and responsibilities'. They report, 'A common finding of effective schools research is that there can be quite substantial gains in effectiveness when the self-esteem of pupils is raised, when they have an active role in the life of the school, and when they are given a share of responsibility for their own learning' (p. 21). This offers a strong pedagogical argument for increased involvement of students in their schools.

In the field of special educational needs, involving pupils in planning and monitoring their own learning or behaviour programmes is considered to be good practice and recommended in a range of guidance from the DfEE. For example, the Code of Practice on the Identification and Assessment of Special Educational Needs (DfE 1994) states that 'Involving children in tracking their own progress within a programme designed to meet their particular learning or behavioural difficulty can contribute to an improved self-image and greater self confidence' (2.36). For pupils identified on the Code of Practice stages of assessment it is recommended that they are involved in drawing up and reviewing their individual education plans. Local Education Authorities are advised to seek the views of pupils undergoing statutory assessment and at annual reviews of statements of special educational needs. For moral and pragmatic reasons as well as sound psychological principles the involvement of children in planning their individual programmes is becoming the norm.

Although pupil involvement in the educational context is not a statutory requirement government guidelines follow the theme of earlier child care legislation. The Children Act 1989 required local authorities to ascertain the wishes and feelings of children looked after and to encourage their participation in assessment, planning and review procedures. Internationally, wider participation rights of children are becoming enshrined in legislation following the 1989 UN Convention on the Rights of the Child, in particular Article 12, which specifies the right for children to express views freely on any matter affecting them. With these significant developments and legislation on human rights expected in the near future the impetus to seek greater involvement of pupils is growing.

Pupils' views should be taken seriously

Acknowledgement of the power of pupil perceptions in providing alternative views of schools to those of adults is gaining ground. Educational psychologists and teachers working in the field of special educational needs have been at the forefront of the developments to enable children's views to be heard. Gersch (1996) reports a range of initiatives to encourage the participation of children in decision-making, including a 'student report' for pupils to comment on their own special educational needs, a student booklet for excluded pupils and a project ('Assessment, Achievement and Action') which placed pupil involvement at the heart of the process for identifying special needs. Two research studies report on the views of children with special educational needs about their experiences of school. Wade and Moore (1993) asked children about teachers, lessons, changing schools, feeling different, getting into trouble and being assessed. Galloway *et al.* (1994) gathered pupil perceptions of the statutory assessment process, revealing some serious misconceptions of the roles of adults. Both studies raise the important issue of the impact pupils' perceptions of their circumstances can have on their performance in school. If a pupil believes she is being assessed to see if her brain is working properly (Galloway *et al.*) she is likely to develop a fatalistic view of her difficulties and a reduced sense of control over the possibility of making progress. Consulting pupils directly not only helps teachers to discover such perceptions but in itself begins to empower learners by allowing them to hear themselves talking about their needs. The experience of having their views heard and valued by an adult or peer can provide an enormous boost to the self-esteem of students who believe they have little control over their own lives, and can make a positive contribution to pupils' capacity to learn effectively.

Impact upon school ethos and culture

Do leaders and managers take account of the views of pupils?

Most school mission statements will make reference to pupils being at the centre of the school aims and objectives. This is reassuring, given that pupils are the *real* clients in education and that we measure our successes largely through quantifying their progress and achievement. How often, though, do pupils have direct dialogue with teachers, managers and leaders in a purposeful, constructive way? What status is afforded to pupil views and issues within school structures? How often do pupil views contribute to the process of change and development in schools? If we were to measure our successes in relation to client satisfaction with, say, the learning environment, preferred styles of learning, range of learning experiences and quality of support and guidance we would be likely to find some alarming discrepancies between what we perceive and what pupils actually think. One school described in

Chapter 4, 'The Practice – Promoting involvement in institutional development', illustrates these discrepancies.

In industry and commerce, change is driven by market forces, through market research and development of new or improved product. The product in education is defined clearly by the government in terms of key stage test results and examination successes and school success is defined largely by these outcomes. This is a perspective on education that needs changing. Handy (1995) refers to 're-framing' as an essential lubricant for change. He suggests that re-framing can give any situation a completely new look, 'It is akin to lateral thinking at times, to using the right side of the brain (the creative pattern-forming side) to complement the more logical left side'. This book suggests that we should be re-framing what constitutes the *product* of education and redefining success from a pupil perspective. It deals with the pupil and his or her success in a more holistic way and provides evidence of pupils who have experienced success in a much wider arena than academic success.

In order to move towards this kind of re-framing, leaders, senior managers and head teachers must do more than articulate visions, convert them into actions, develop effective action plans and monitor, evaluate and review their progress. They must be involved in the dynamics of organisations, be sensitive to the pressures and forces which are exerted by people in organisations to support or block progress and change. They have to be able to measure the temperature of organisations, know where the hot or cool spots are, know how to dampen the fire or melt the ice. A truly successful school is often less about the systems that are in place and more about the quality of communication, the quality of relationships and the feelings of empowerment in people within the organisation. Fullan (1992) asserts that 'the challenge is to improve education in the only way it can be – through the day-to-day actions of empowered individuals'. This book suggests that pupils have a place as empowered people in learning organisations, that the voices of pupils should be heard by teachers and managers and that their views should contribute effectively to the processes of change, development and improvement in our schools.

Questioning and reflective schools

Schools most likely to take account of the views and opinions of their pupils will be those where a culture of collaboration and collegiality exist. 'Questioning' schools, where inquiry is a part of the teaching and learning process, encourage leaders, teachers and pupils to be learners and to reflect on their strengths and weaknesses. By so doing, teachers and pupils will be focused on practice and on ways to improve it.

Where questioning schools deal with problematic issues successfully, practical and creative solutions will be found, communicated, supported and facilitated by managers. These schools will be seeking to encourage:

- ways in which pupil views of practice can impact on leadership views;
- processes whereby pupil views will be channelled systematically into school development planning;

- all staff to listen and respond positively to pupil views, needs and rights;
- pupils as leaders through the teaching of key skills, thinking and problem-solving skills.

Schools where collaborative practice is encouraged and nurtured will have a strong sense of community and of everyone's place and value within the community. There will be evidence of:

- staff working with pupils – designing, implementing, reviewing the curriculum through consideration of the individual and collective views and needs of pupils;
- development of whole-school aspects, for example cross-curricular skills, study skills, thinking skills, personal and social education, citizenship.

In the following section, 'Promoting inclusion', we deal with the wider aspects of collaborative practice leading to the meaningful implementation of inclusion.

Are teachers risk-takers?

Many of us will remember teachers at school who used the same set of notes for each teaching group, year after year using the same examples, anecdotes and references. Those that stand out in our memories were unpredictable; they used different methods to arrive at conclusions, and encouraged pupils to be active participants in learning and to express views and opinions about themselves, their lives and their school. We may have called these teachers 'risky', because they took risks which sometimes worked and were sometimes unsuccessful, but which were almost always exciting to experience and rarely produced negative, disaffected responses from pupils.

Covey (1992) promotes the involvement of people in creating change. He states:

the down side of involvement is risk. Whenever you involve people in the problem, you risk losing control. It is so much easier, simpler, and safer – and seemingly so much more efficient – not to involve others, but simply to tell them, to direct them, to advise them. (p. 218)

Being a risk-taker does not align itself easily with being a teacher. Prescriptive curriculum structures, proliferation of rules, systems, checks and controls along with the need to be effective at maintaining discipline and an orderly community lead many teachers to favour a direct, didactic style which demands relatively little response from pupils. The emphasis on maintenance of power and control lies firmly with the teacher but often restricts the creative aspects of teaching and learning and most certainly restricts the learner. Fullan and Hargreaves (1992) suggest that risks are possible, and even preferable to accepting the status quo, as long as they are positive and likely to succeed. This book examines the way teachers and others develop positive approaches which encourage pupil autonomy and control over learning, through:

- allowing pupils to lead;
- listening to pupils' views;

- affording pupils respect;
- treating pupils as partners, while maintaining boundaries;
- staff treating themselves as learners;
- framing questions from a pupil perspective;
- concentrating on developing interpersonal skills in pupils;
- dealing with pupil conflict through empowerment by involving pupils in setting and tracking targets for IEPs, use of circle-time, thinking skills strategies, pupil groups such as student councils;
- personal reflection on teaching and learning styles;
- consciously letting go of superficial control and authority.

Schools described in this book conclude that many of the risks taken during the 'Involving Pupils' project have led to positive outcomes for pupils, staff and learning organisations.

Promoting inclusion

What is inclusion?

As the *Programme of Action* (DfEE 1998) clearly states, 'inclusion is a process not a fixed state'. We suggest that this process must involve more than the mere relocation of pupils from specialist contexts into mainstream schools. For the purposes of this book, we define educational inclusion as a process in which all members of the school community constantly challenge themselves to reconceptualise their policies, their practices, their roles and their perceptions about the people around them in order to provide an ever more effective education for an ever more diverse range of learners.

In a more inclusive future, it will no longer be acceptable for mainstream schools to continue to deny places to pupils with special educational needs simply because established practices, structures and procedures are designed to meet the needs of only a certain proportion of potential pupils. Where learners, in the opinion of professionals, parents and the young people themselves, are likely to benefit from education in a mainstream setting, the *Programme of Action* recommends that schools should ask themselves: 'what action would be needed, by whom, to make this possible?' In other words, a school which seeks to become more inclusive must be prepared to change the ways in which it works in order to respond more effectively to the wide-ranging and individual needs of pupils. What is more, we suggest, the inclusive school will subject its ethos, its curriculum and all the structures and procedures which support teaching and learning to ongoing review and revision in order constantly to aspire to maintaining and extending inclusivity. In committing themselves to a rolling cycle of development in this way, schools can become what Skrtic (1991) calls 'problem-solving organisations that configure themselves around uncertain work'. In a more inclusive system, therefore, pupils experiencing difficulties will be welcomed in schools because they provide the challenges which drive improvement.

Conceptualising achievement

If schools are to embrace uncertainty in this way, there will be a need to develop new measures of effectiveness. These measures will reach beyond school performance tables based on the outcomes of standardised assessments and examination results and begin to reveal a sense of the 'value added' by inclusive schools for all pupils, including those experiencing difficulties of various kinds. Appropriate measures of the effectiveness of inclusive schools will involve the certification of a variety of forms of achievement beyond academic success in relation to the formal curriculum. Schools may consider validating progress in developing thinking skills, for example, or key skills in learning to learn, to communicate or to work with others. In this book, we will propose that inclusive schools will also want to evaluate their effectiveness by consolidating ways of measuring:

- pupils' satisfaction with the school experience;
- pupils' personal growth and the development of enhanced self-esteem;
- the active involvement of pupils in a range of social and educational processes.

Special schools and units, in collaboration with their mainstream colleagues, will have an important role to play in this process. They may focus on preparing pupils for reintegration and on providing a curriculum with educational and social inclusion as explicit outcomes. This means that inclusive schools will provide a whole curriculum which includes the subjects of the National Curriculum (and a full range of opportunities for all pupils to demonstrate achievement in relation to that curriculum) but which also acknowledges other priorities. These priorities may be met through schemes of work in areas such as citizenship or personal, social and health education and through activities designed explicitly to help all pupils to learn how to learn. They may also be addressed through the goals and targets negotiated and agreed between staff, pupils and parents in the individual education planning process established in response to the *Code of Practice* (DfE 1994). These targets will ensure that opportunities to develop key skills in a range of contexts across the curriculum are identified and that pupils are actively involved in making the most of such opportunities.

Narrow approaches to the curriculum and its assessment and certification will not be sustainable in inclusive schools. Fortunately, the *Programme of Action* supports this prospect by suggesting that inclusion demands 'imaginative approaches to the curriculum'. In particular, schools are encouraged to explore new flexibilities in the curriculum at Key Stage 4 where, it is suggested, 'alternative approaches' may involve links with Colleges of Further Education and the voluntary sector in order to encourage pupils to realise the links between school and adult life, including work.

This is not to suggest that schools will need to compromise standards in working towards increased inclusivity. Sebba and Sachdev's (1997) review of international research reveals that the majority of pupils make 'the same or more progress', achieving comparable standards or better, in inclusive classrooms as in traditional mainstream classes. Further, pupils with special educational needs also gain from the experience of being included, particularly in terms of enhanced skills in language and reading, skills for life and, interestingly, skills for learning. As we have already suggested above in our comments on pupil empowerment and enhanced self-esteem, we do not wish to underplay the extent to which the agendas for empowerment and achievement coexist in tension with one another. Neither do we wish to imply that working towards inclusivity entails accepting lower standards. On the contrary, the following chapters recognise the very real challenges faced by staff and pupils in reformulating practice in accordance with more inclusive priorities. In particular, we acknowledge the challenges faced by pupils when confronting imminent reintegration into mainstream schools where they may have experienced difficulties in the past.

Pupil perspectives

If reintegration is to be successful under these circumstances, it must be undertaken in close collaboration between staff and pupils. In the following pages, we give a number of examples of pupils negotiating targets with staff and working steadily towards reintegration or full inclusion as an explicit outcome. It is important that pupils have a real sense of ownership over targets which are as important to their futures, and, potentially, as threatening, as these are likely to be. Not all the pupils in the examples that follow regard reintegration as a prized goal. Some of them will have been damaged by their experiences of the mainstream and their perceived 'failures' in that context; many of them will have come to depend, to some extent or another, upon the increased levels of tuition, support and, often, involvement which they have found in specialist contexts. We would suggest, therefore, that schools should collaborate with pupils primarily out of a sense of natural justice – because pupils have a right to be involved in plans, policies and decisions which affect them so profoundly; to express their preferences; and to be enabled to make informed choices. We would also argue, with Sammons *et al.* (1995) and Ainscow (1999), that provision is unlikely to improve and to become more inclusive unless schools learn to listen to the voices of pupils. As Ainscow says, 'arguably the critical group to which involvement needs to be extended is the pupils themselves'. Ainscow goes on to define inclusion:

> as a process of increasing the participation of pupils in, and reducing their exclusion from, the cultures, curricula and communities of their local schools. (p. 218)

It becomes inevitable, therefore, that special and mainstream schools will, in a more inclusive future, be working much more closely together in order to reduce what Ainscow calls the 'barriers to pupil participation' at a number of levels. The *Programme of Action* acknowledges this and asserts that specialist provision of one kind or another will form an integral part of an 'increasingly inclusive education system'. This is not to say that special schools and units will be able simply to remain as they are. Our contention is that all providers, mainstream and specialist, will need to re-frame what they do and the context in which the work of education is done. In the following chapters, we will suggest that this means that mainstream schools should take account of some of the understandings and strategies arrived at by the specialist sector. It also means that special schools and units should explore, in much greater depth, their relationship with the mainstream curriculum, mainstream approaches and mainstream concerns, including the development of key skills and thinking skills.

Working collaboratively

One of the key issues in developing inclusive policy revolves around the need to reduce rates of exclusion as well as opening up mainstream schools to pupils who would traditionally have been taught in the specialist sector. The *Programme of Action* proposes that special schools and units should make themselves available for pupils on short-term placements and puts forward the idea of mainstream schools and the specialist sector offering dual registration to some pupils. If staff are to share responsibility for educating pupils on this sort of level, the processes of collaboration between the mainstream and specialist contexts will have to be extremely sophisticated and driven by an ongoing commitment on the part of senior managers and governors, to cooperative approaches to problem-solving.

This is a model of collaboration which goes far beyond any models of integration we have yet seen. Links between mainstream and special schools which have depended upon personal contacts and the goodwill of individual teachers are inevitably frail. Even where effective systems for the exchange of pupil information are established, these usually entail some form of division of responsibility between two contexts for learning. The *Programme of Action* suggests that working towards inclusive practices might entail colleagues in special schools acting as sources of advice and expertise for mainstream colleagues. We would hope that any such arrangements would be reciprocal and we would take this debate further by promoting the value of shared development.

In this model, school communities in the mainstream and specialist sectors would work together to reconceptualise what they do, why they do it and who they do it for. This would lead to shared policy-making and curriculum development. It would facilitate the easy flow of insight and expertise across personal and professional boundaries, making practice more responsive and effective. It would mean governors, staff, families and pupils working together in close, critical partnerships, supporting one another, reviewing their work together and striving constantly to meet their shared responsibilities for learning and whole-pupil development across the full range of pupil diversity. It would also lead to the reconfiguration of the concepts of 'special educational needs' themselves. We suggest, with Hart (1996), that thinking needs to move away from the paradigm in which difficulties with learning are identified solely within the learner. This process leads inexorably towards the transfer of responsibility for 'problem' pupils to specialist staff working in specialist domains. Inclusive practices which are fully collaborative will begin to re-frame teaching and learning as areas of responsibility which are shared between staff, parents and pupils in a cooperative endeavour to the mutual benefit of all parties.

We do not suggest that inclusive practices will make difficulties disappear. We argue rather that individual needs are most effectively met through teamwork and that everyone in the school community, including the pupils themselves, needs to acknowledge the importance of collaboration, critical friendships and learning from one another. These processes will help all members of the school community to become more aware of what they are doing and of their own strengths and difficulties. Those who embrace the uncertainty of a problem-solving culture will need to be committed to re-framing their roles and reconstituting their understandings through reflection, review, revision and re-evaluation. Through collaboration, staff, pupils and families will find themselves better able to offer one another support while subjecting the work of the school community to a constant process of challenge and change.

A guide to the materials and their potential uses

We offer here a brief guide to the materials and the ways in which they might be used. The book covers a significant body of school-based research and is intended as a source of ideas, approaches, case studies, information, resources and references in order to assist schools in reflection on their own practice and in developing new practices.

Who are we writing for?

The book is aimed at those involved in developing provision for pupils and students with a wide range of special educational needs, including:

- school staff – teachers, learning support assistants, and other support staff working in special school or inclusive settings;
- school managers and governors;
- advisers, inspectors and educational psychologists;
- professionals in the health, social services and voluntary sectors working with clients with special educational needs and their families;
- students in higher education and school staff pursuing further professional development.

How do we think you might use the book?

The book is divided into four major sections:

- the 'Introduction', which describes the project and three major themes which are developed throughout the book;
- 'The Practice', which describes the work of the seven participating schools in

detail, under three main themes – pupils as partners; teaching thinking skills; promoting involvement in institutional development;

- 'Evaluation and Implications', which identifies the outcomes of the project and their impact on schools;
- 'Conclusions and Audit Check', which opens out challenges and opportunities for readers, and includes an audit checklist for use in schools.

The book also contains examples of proformas and samples of resources and materials used and developed in the project schools, with relevant contacts and addresses. Further details of those resources shown in italics are provided in the 'Resources' section.

The book is structured in this way to enable the reader to follow any of the strands through the book, to read one chapter or aspect in isolation, or to dip in and out of chapters as required. Although we hope that many readers will wish to read the book from cover to cover, it is possible that certain aspects will be of more interest and use to individual readers.

The book therefore might be used to:

- review systems and processes of pupil involvement in individual education planning;
- review pupil involvement in assessment, recording, reporting and annual reviews;
- develop more pupil-focused approaches to teaching and learning;
- develop pupil involvement in school issues and decision-making;
- examine ways in which pupil self-esteem might be raised;
- develop creative approaches to reducing disaffection;
- help develop more independent learners.

Throughout the book we refer to *pupils* when describing learners at Key Stages 1, 2 and 3. We refer to *students* when describing learners at Key Stage 4 and beyond. Where there is a multi-disciplinary dimension to the work described, we sometimes also refer to *young people*. For the purposes of this book, where the word *school* is used it will refer to the schools *and* the 'unit' participating in the project.

Where widely known acronyms are used, the first reference to the name will be written in full, followed by the acronym in parentheses. From this point onwards the acronym only may be used.

In the following three chapters we describe the work of participating schools during the 'Involving Pupils' project. The chapters deal with the following themes.

- Pupils as partners: which examines ways in which participating schools worked on promoting involvement of individual pupils in their learning;
- Teaching thinking skills: which describes the work of participating schools whose main focus was the empowerment of pupils and students through the teaching of thinking skills programmes;
- Promoting involvement in institutional development: which describes the way in which participating schools worked with groups of pupils and students to involve them more in the decision-making processes of the school.

Each chapter contains references to, and descriptions of, the work of various participating schools. Extracts taken directly from the text of final project reports are printed in italics. Examples of materials or proformas are boxed as Figures or presented as appendices.

CHAPTER 2

The Practice – Pupils as partners

This section explores a range of developments in three of the participating schools which entail:

- agreeing priorities, setting targets and planning teaching and learning in partnership with individual pupils;
- pupil involvement in assessment, individual education plans and the Annual Review cycle.

These approaches build on one of the themes which informed the development of the *Code of Practice* (DfE 1994) and one of the key principles of the 'Involving Pupils' project. This section describes work in progress, and readers will find notes about outcomes to date as well as intentions for future developments in Chapter 5, 'Evaluation and Implications'.

Introduction

The *Code of Practice on the Identification and Assessment of Special Educational Needs* was introduced at least partly in an attempt to overcome some of the structural and administrative problems which had become endemic since the implementation of the 1981 Education Act (Audit Commission/HMI 1992). The *Code* was also built around some of the principles of consultation and negotiation which had informed the Education Act of 1981 and the Children Act of 1989. The resulting tensions, between the establishment of formal systems designed to clarify and expedite the processes entailed in supporting pupils with a wide range of specified special educational needs and the encouragement of new forms of partnership, have meant that the *Code* has not been easily or evenly assimilated into the working lives of schools (Garner 1995, Hornby 1995). As a result, the *Code* itself is being subjected to revision.

The original *Code of Practice* is very clear about the role that pupils with special educational needs should have in their own learning, however. As we have seen, schools are asked to consider how they:

- involve pupils in decision-making processes;
- determine the pupil's level of participation, taking into account approaches to assessment and intervention which are suitable for his or her age, ability and past experiences;
- record pupils' views in identifying their difficulties, setting goals, agreeing a development strategy, monitoring and reviewing progress;
- involve pupils in implementing education plans.

(DfE 1994, para. 2.37, p. 15)

As Ramjhun (1995) notes, it is the intention of the *Code* that school staff should 'ascertain the child's views, wishes and perceptions and involve him in the implementation of the IEP' or individual education plan. If this level of pupil involvement, in identifying strengths and weaknesses, setting targets for improvement, and developing and monitoring individual education plans, is seen as problematic in mainstream schools, it may certainly appear daunting for those who work with pupils who experience significant difficulties in their learning. The *Code* offers some general guidance here:

> the adults closest to the child have a responsibility to establish to the best of their ability the wishes and feelings of the child, for example by interpreting the child's behaviour in different settings as a measure of the child's preferences. However they are ascertained, the wishes and feelings of the child have a separate identity and, even though they may overlap or coincide with the views of others, the LEA may wish to have the child's views set out separately from those of the parents and professionals.

(DfE 1994, para. 3.120, p. 78)

For staff in some specialist contexts, coming to terms with the notion that the principles of the *Code* apply to them as well as to their mainstream colleagues brings not inconsiderable difficulties. While many of the professionally driven systems and procedures outlined in the *Code* are familiar, and, indeed, have their origins firmly in established special school practice, the theme of pupil involvement presents a novel challenge for many. Others, who have been developing their practice in the light of guidance on the preparation and presentation of Records of Achievement (DES 1990, SEAC 1990, Tilstone 1991, Lawson 1992, Rushton and Harwick 1994) and Progress Files (DfEE 1997) for instance, may feel less daunted about the possibility of consultation and negotiation in the classroom. Most special schools, and perhaps particularly those for whom the notion of a partnership with parents (DES 1981) is still to be realised, may have reacted with some surprise at the *Code's* suggestion that:

> wherever possible, pupils should also be actively involved in the review process, including all or part of the review meeting, and should be encouraged to give their views of their progress during the previous year; discuss any difficulties encountered; and share their hopes and aspirations for the future.

(DfE 1994, para. 6.15, p. 110)

While all pupils, at all ages, are to be involved in decision-making processes at all levels, the reality of involvement and consultation should become more tangible, according to the *Code of Practice*, for young people with special educational needs in their teenage years.

> The views of young people themselves should be sought and recorded wherever possible in any assessment, reassessment or review during the years of transition. Some young people may wish to express these views through a trusted professional, family, independent advocate or adviser, the Named Person or through an officer of the authority. Effective arrangements for transition will involve young people themselves addressing issues of:
>
> - personal development
> - self advocacy
> - the development of a positive self image
> - awareness of the implications of any long term health problem or disability
> - the growth of personal autonomy and the acquisition of independent living skills.
>
> (DfE 1994, para. 6.59, p. 122)

The introduction here of concepts of citizen and self-advocacy (Tyne 1994, Mittler 1996) echoes Tisdall's (1994) view that 'young people themselves, supported and encouraged by the disability advocacy groups, need to define their own goals'. Language like this, taken together with the drive to promote personal autonomy and independence skills, takes the debate beyond a reconsideration of practice in terms of assessment, record-keeping and reporting. *The Code of Practice* has real implications for curriculum design and development:

> curriculum planning should focus on activities which encourage students to review and reflect upon their own experiences and wishes and to formulate and articulate their views.
>
> (DfE 1994, para. 6.60, p. 122)

These words will be seen to have a very direct impact upon the curriculum for pupils with special educational needs in Key Stage 4 and beyond, but they should affect the curriculum for pupils with learning difficulties at all age stages. There is no reason to believe that pupils will suddenly become able to 'formulate and articulate their views' at the age of 14. Indeed, as Tisdall states, 'a considerable problem of the transitional process is the unpreparedness of disabled young people actually to make transitional decisions'. If the process of shared curriculum review and planning is to be meaningful for young adults, then the curriculum for younger pupils will have to change in order to promote the skills, attitudes and understandings which will make this decision-making possible and professionals will have to equip themselves to hear, to acknowledge, to respect and to act upon the wishes and aspirations of pupils.

The notion of teaching pupils skills for thinking and learning is addressed in detail in the following section of this book. Suffice it to say here that, as Ramjhun (1995) notes, pupils' individual education plans should focus on 'one or two priority areas of difficulty' which are considered, by staff, pupils and parents, to be a 'priority for action'. The DfEE (1998, and see also DfEE/QCA 1999) has emphasised that individual education plans should focus on 'three or four short-term targets' for each pupil and that these targets will typically relate to 'key skills such as communication, literacy, numeracy, behaviour and social skills' rather than subject content. The *National Curriculum* (DfEE/QCA 1999) lists sets of thinking skills and key skills which we give in full as Appendix 1. Where pupils experience difficulties with their learning, we suggest that these sets of key and thinking skills might provide a useful starting point when staff, pupils and parents come together in order to discuss priority areas to be addressed as targets in pupils' individual education plans. It is also interesting to note that targets of this kind transcend subject boundaries and will enable colleagues from a range of professional backgrounds to contribute to the development and implementation of pupils' individual education plans.

Establishing priorities in partnership with individual pupils

Example 1: Assessment and planning at Longview Unit

Young people with mental health problems who experience difficulties in their mainstream schools are referred to Longview Unit by their local Child and Family Consultation Service (CFCS). The first assessment meeting focuses on determining, among other things, the young people's own views of their difficulties and of the help that they feel they need. Targets for admission are discussed and made clear to the young people and their families so that they can make the decision as to whether to use the service provided by the Unit or not. Under relatively unusual circumstances, powers under the Mental Health Act 1983 are invoked and young people forfeit the right to make a voluntary commitment to a period of involvement at Longview Unit. However, the preferred course of events secures pupil involvement in decision-making from the outset.

On admission to Longview, a detailed assessment is undertaken by a key worker in order to look at a range of 'whole pupil' issues such as:

- moods and affective responses;
- interactions with other people;
- sleep patterns and diet.

Over the next few weeks, this initial assessment is used as a basis for drawing up a care plan. Because of its role as a unit for young people experiencing a range of acute, severe and/or chronic mental health difficulties, practice at Longview Unit has a strong multi-disciplinary foundation and staff are committed to the principles of inter-agency collaboration. The education programme is viewed as providing one more opportunity for therapeutic change within the overall Longview experience and the therapeutic regime is designed in such a way that each young person can move between the education and nursing strands, depending upon individual need, mental state and capacity at any moment in time. Multi-disciplinary programmes of care are individually negotiated and planned and are reviewed with the youngsters on a regular basis. The care plan may be produced by the key worker and then discussed with the pupil; developed in collaboration between the pupil and the key worker; or written initially by the pupil and then discussed with the key worker. Whatever the balance of responsibility in these negotiations, both pupil and professional will normally agree the contents of the care plan and both parties will sign it. Again, there may be circumstances under which individual pupils refuse to sign up to their care plans and adults are forced to take responsibility for initiating implementation. On these exceptional occasions, the nature of the pupil's disagreement with the care plan is carefully noted and attempts to re-establish consensus are made at a later stage. Since there are no set periods for the review of the care plan, this opportunity may be presented to the young person on a daily basis. Other care plans, depending on the pupil's most urgently pressing needs, are reviewed each week or fortnightly. The period of review may be extended to three weeks as any sense of crisis or immediate risk recedes.

Each pupil's care plan is reviewed by a multi-disciplinary team, led by the consultant psychiatrist. In preparation for this meeting, each pupil is given an opportunity each week to record their views on their care plan and their progress in written form. These notes are presented to the review meeting and responses will be fed back to the pupil by a designated person. The young people themselves can ask to attend their review meeting in order to ask questions or make comments or requests.

At the outset of the 'Involving Pupils' project, therefore, staff at Longview already regarded themselves as being 'extremely successful in involving youngsters in their everyday programmes and in the overall Longview experience'. The following practices were described, in summary, as being standard within the unit:

- *Young people are involved in the admission assessment process and, in instances where their mental state makes this feasible, they agree to enter Longview for treatment.*
- *Young people are involved in the drawing up of the multi-disciplinary care plans and in regular reviews.*
- *Young people are expected to contribute in person or in writing to their reviews and case conferences on a weekly and six weekly basis respectively so that their views can be considered.*
- *Within the classroom area, young people are involved in negotiating their individual education plans and reviewing them on a regular basis.*
- *Young people are involved in the process of setting their discharge date and in negotiating their future placements.*

Staff at Longview have set themselves standards, which are audited and evaluated regularly using the *Dynamic Standard Setting System* (a framework for achieving quality improvement – see 'Resources' section), to ensure that these targets for the involvement of young people continue to be reached. Staff were also aware, however, that other assessment and recording policies within the education department needed to be evaluated in order to promote increased pupil involvement. For example, if a young person's mental state makes it possible, Longview undertakes a comprehensive academic assessment process on admission, which includes application of such tests as:

- *Macmillan Reading Test*
- *NFER Comprehension Test*
- *NFER Reading Test*
- *Profile of Maths Skills*
- *Richmond Tests of Basic Skills*
- *Reading-Miscue Analysis.*

These materials (see 'Resources' section for full details), when compared with details received from the mainstream school, allow staff at Longview to develop an academic baseline for each young person. This information might provide some sense of the effects of mental health on learning, but it began to be regarded as unreliable and as allowing limited pupil feedback and involvement. In joining the 'Involving Pupils' project, staff at Longview perceived an overriding need for disadvantaged, disaffected and vulnerable young people to be empowered to take control of learning again for themselves, developing skills that will be relevant and purposeful to them in the future. It was anticipated that this form of empowerment would not only facilitate the therapeutic process itself but also help the young people to reintegrate back into mainstream education at the end of their involvement with Longview.

A member of Longview's staff therefore studied to become qualified to Level A in psychometric testing. This enabled the unit to add the following materials (see 'Resources' section for details) to its assessment toolkit:

- *Ravens Matrices (non-verbal)*
- *British Picture Vocabulary Scale (verbal)*
- *The Adolescent Coping Scale.*

With these additions and increased testing skills, staff at Longview can now identify any discrepancy between a young person's verbal and non-verbal skills. Further explorations may reveal if, for example, a specific learning difficulty might have impacted on the young person's particular mental health difficulties. This might lead the Educational Psychologist to carry out further assessments so that recommendations can be made to the mainstream school. Longview can also look at how the young person tackles problems, highlighting the positive strategies already used, but also indicating approaches that could be developed in order to enable a student to function more effectively in the future. All this information is discussed with the young people themselves and integrated into their individual education plans. Using the recently extended range of assessment materials, staff at Longview are increasingly able to use the individual education planning process in order to set specific targets for the use of key cognitive skills and strategies that each young person will address in the classroom setting with their key teacher. This work is described in more detail in Chapter 3 'Teaching thinking skills'. However, it is already clear that individual education plans at Longview, in line with the recommendations of the *Programme of Action* (DfEE 1998), now include an increasing number of targets specifically related to thinking skills and problem-solving.

Negotiating targets with individual pupils

Example 1: Setting targets at The Heath School

Staff at The Heath School had two overall aims at the outset of the 'Involving Pupils' project:

- to raise pupils' awareness of the targets within their statements of special educational needs and subsequent annual reviews;
- to improve the level of involvement the pupils have in the process of target setting and evaluation as part of their whole educational plan.

These aims flowed from a recognition that pupils tended to have low levels of awareness of their own statements or of the targets being set for them. Staff realised that they would have to make significant changes to their own attitudes and practices if pupils were to become more involved. Two further aims were therefore developed for the project:

- to increase the level of staff awareness of the contents of statements of special educational needs and of the relationships between statements and annual reviews;
- to improve colleagues' communication skills and confidence levels with a focus on enabling them to negotiate and establish targets and then to evaluate any progress in partnership with pupils.

These subsidiary aims had enormous implications for staff training. Project participants at The Heath School recognised that they were about to embark on a project which would result in whole-school change and sought the appropriate support and consensus, as their report reveals:

At this point it was critical to receive the backing of the senior management team. In order to receive this support it was very important to be able to convince them that an integral part of the project was to make the whole school benefit from the resultant work.

Staff participating in the 'Involving Pupils' project at The Heath School decided to begin with a small-scale trial of their ideas. Four pupils who were involved in the school's reintegration programme were selected as a trial group. Staff had a sense that these pupils might be willing and eager to become more involved in setting their own targets and that successful participation in the project might help to provide firm evidence that they were ready to be accepted back into the mainstream of schooling.

At this early stage, the four case study pupils were provided with regular meeting times with key staff in order to enable them to discuss their targets. These targets focused on reintegration into the mainstream setting and clear action plans, with stated review dates, were established very carefully in cooperation with the pupils. We provide an example of the proforma that the pupils completed alongside the support staff in the pilot study as Figure 2.1 and Appendix 2.

It was difficult for staff at The Heath School to quantify the impact that involvement in this target setting and evaluation process had upon pupils. The four case study pupils all made significant progress but this might have been prompted by the sense of motivation and achievement resulting simply from renewed attendance at a mainstream school. However, all four case study pupils and the staff involved reported that they regarded the process of sharing and evaluating targets as worthwhile. As a direct consequence of this positive feedback, project participants set out to try to raise staff and pupil awareness of individual targets throughout The Heath School.

MY ACTION PLAN

What am I like now?

What do I want to achieve?

My target(s):

What will I do in order to achieve my target(s)?

How will I know when I have succeeded?

What evidence will I show others in order to share in my success?

EVALUATION

I have been working on my target for . . . . . . weeks.

I feel I need/don't need more time to work on my target (*delete as appropriate*).

Signed: . . . . (pupil)   Date: . . . .

Figure 2.1 A prototype format for shared target setting at The Heath School

This stage of the project involved participating staff in a time-consuming search of school documents. The personal file of every pupil in the school was located and details of the targets in their statements of special educational needs were extracted. Staff decided to present each pupil's targets in a user-friendly format on a single sheet of paper. Other additional personal information was also noted on this sheet and two copies were made. One copy was placed in a newly created central file in the main school office as a record of the current targets for every pupil in the school. The second copy was attached to the pupil's personal file, used regularly by all staff for everyday record keeping. The project participants hoped that this would, in itself, raise awareness of the targets since they would be clearly visible to all concerned.

As a result of these early initiatives, staff and pupils did begin to take more notice of priorities for learning based on statements. The majority of the aims written into statements of special educational need when pupils arrive at The Heath School focus on behaviour. These behavioural aims tend to be broad and general. Using these broad aims in order to develop good quality short-term targets for pupils' individual education plans requires skill, ingenuity and experience. The aims need to be broken down into more manageable and achievable elements which can be implemented in the short term and evaluated annually.

One of the purposes of the individual education plan is to provide a structure for setting and evaluating short-term targets for and with pupils. The 'Involving Pupils' project encouraged The Heath School to use individual education plans as an integral part of the planning and evaluation procedures designed to meet the needs of all pupils. The flow diagram at Figure 2.2 was developed in order to show staff and the pupils how the individual education plan fits in with other target setting and evaluation systems in use at the school.

As project participants discussed the introduction of individual education plans with their colleagues, it became clear that staff would need support and training in order to be able to engage pupils in discussions focused on:

- areas of success;
- perceived difficulties;
- potential for future development

and then to negotiate shared targets for individual education plans.

The senior management team at The Heath School supported requests for two separate forms of professional development and two training days were set aside, one for each of the following aspects:

- work on the skills needed in order to record, monitor and evaluate targets;
- consideration of the communication skills needed in order to elicit responses from pupils and involve them in establishing their own targets (see Figure 2.2).

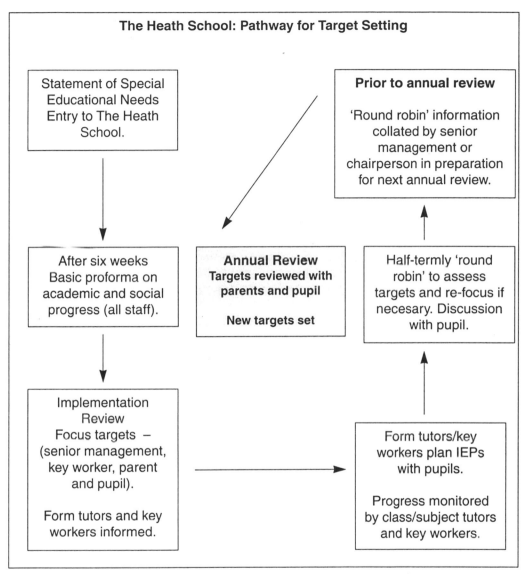

Figure 2.2 The whole-school pathway for reviewing targets at The Heath School

As a result of working together around these issues, the school has adopted the philosophy of developing targets with SMART characteristics:

Specific
Manageable
Achievable
Relevant
Time-limited.

This framework has allowed the school to provide a consistent approach to target setting throughout the school. A sample of the targets provided for one year group is set out in Figure 2.3.

Pupil 1
1 To arrive to lesson on time.
2 To address members of staff politely and appropriately (Mr, Mrs, Miss, first
   name).
3 To attempt to read when asked.

Pupil 2
1 To use a ruler and pencil for diagrams.
2 To share with others in practical lessons and out of class sessions.
3 To arrive on time to lessons.

Pupil 3
1 To attend assembly and/or leave quietly when he's had enough.
2 To use appropriate language in class.

Pupil 4
1 To respect others working by not making 'sound effects' when in class.
2 To finish the task set completely when in class.
3 To make a positive comment to people during the lesson.

Figure 2.3 Sample targets from individual education plans at The Heath School

Involving pupils in the individual education planning process

Example 1: Developing individual education plans at The Heath School

Although developing skills in setting SMART targets was a necessary step for staff at The Heath School to take (see above), it was not in itself sufficient. Project participants undertook further steps in order to raise the profile of pupils' targets and to promote the involvement of the pupils themselves. As part of the process of improving practice in setting targets at The Heath School, all staff were given training in an approach called *Solution Focused Brief Therapy* (Rhodes and Ajmal 1995 – see also 'Resources' section). This provided one structure for discussing progress and coming to agreements about possible individual education plan targets with pupils.

The training in 'Brief Therapy' provided the staff with the confidence needed to start work on involving pupils more meaningfully in the development of their individual education plans (IEPs). The next part of the project focused on trying to embed the skills that staff had gained during training into day-to-day practice. As project participants at The Heath School noted:

It was important to be realistic. The introduction of IEPs, shared by all, was to be a major change for both the school staff and the pupils themselves. One of the most significant factors was deciding who would take overall management of the IEPs. After much deliberation it was decided that the most logical person would be the form tutor, closely supported by the pupil's key worker. This involved a change in role for the form tutors and the creation of yet more work for them. The new role was accepted by form tutors, though not without some trepidation.

Staff at The Heath School decided to introduce the new procedures with a pilot group consisting of two pupils per year group. There were good reasons for this decision. A pilot scheme would allow staff to identify problem areas in the proposed structures and give time to develop modifications before putting the whole process into operation for all pupils. It would also allow staff to work with a manageable number of pupils while they became familiar with the proposed processes. In this way, the skills learnt on the training days could be put into practice gradually; adequate time could be taken while staff became relaxed in their new ways of working; and small numbers of pupils would not present too daunting a prospect in the early stages of the innovation.

It was agreed that form tutors and key workers would use a newly designed common format when involving pupils in the setting of targets within individual education plans. The original format, which is provided here as Figure 2.4, helped to focus participants on a number of significant points for discussion. An updated version is also offered as Appendix 3 for interested readers to copy and use.

It was ultimately agreed that pupils at The Heath School should work towards a small set of up to three individual education plan targets during any one half term. Staff decided to develop separate recording methods and processes for 'in class' (during teaching time) and 'out of class' (during non-teaching time) targets.

Name:... Date of Birth: ....
Date Targets Set: .... Review Date: ....
Strengths
Areas for Development

	Target	Support Strategies	Success Criteria	Evaluation/ Review
1.				
2.				
3.				

Parental comments

Pupil comments

Figure 2.4 Format for individual education plans at The Heath School

Achievements in relation to 'in class' targets have proved to be much easier to evaluate than those relating to 'out of class' targets since pupils are not so closely observed during the 'out of class' sessions.

It is now common practice at The Heath School to review 'in class' individual education plan targets with each pupil at the end of every lesson. Class teachers are responsible for recording significant information and, with this system, feedback to the pupil is immediate and individual. In order to maintain consistency across the school, classroom staff adopted a collaborative approach to designing a record sheet for the 'in class' targets. The intention is that this sheet can be used as both a prompt to remind individual pupils about their agreed targets during an activity and as a means of record keeping at the end of a lesson. Targets which are not relevant to the 'in class' situation are not included on this prompt sheet.

The record-keeping template ensures that the targets appear adjacent to the recording boxes when the two sheets are presented side by side in a class folder or a record book. Ticks and dates can be placed in a small box when a target is reached and a larger space is provided for more extended comments and notes about pupil progress.

Staff at The Heath School have found this to be an effective method of collecting data in relation to 'in class' targets. Monitoring and recording progress in relation to the 'out of class' targets has proved to be more problematic since carrying round a folder containing the relevant information for all pupils during these periods, while on lunch duty for example, would be cumbersome and impractical for the staff. Key workers therefore often actively involve pupils in the monitoring, recording and review processes relating to 'out of class' targets. For example, pupils may be expected to carry a prompt card or a proforma with them as a reminder of their 'out of class' targets. They may be made responsible for handing these documents over to be signed by a member of staff at the end of the session. This sort of pupil involvement has many advantages:

- pupils become more aware of their targets and their own progress towards them;
- pupils develop ownership of record-keeping processes and outcomes;
- pupils collect good quality data during 'out of class' sessions which may be deliberately unstructured and less well observed by staff;
- pupils receive immediate feedback in the form of praise or further encouragement just as they do in 'in class' situations.

A record of each pupil's 'out of class' targets is maintained in the daily record file, where it can act as a prompt to both care staff and teaching staff, and record keeping in relation to 'out of class' targets can also be linked to the school's behaviour support programmes. Although the pupils themselves are involved in agreeing their 'out of class' targets with their key workers, staff are responsible for focusing targets so as to ensure that it will be possible to measure and record any progress made. Having good quality targets has a great influence on record-keeping and assessment. Staff at The Heath School quickly realised, during the pilot phases of this project, that targets written in accordance with SMART criteria (see above) support focused evaluation. Recording meaningful data in relation to targets which are not SMART can be very difficult. Staff at The Heath School regard the development of focused target setting as a critical element in the success of their system.

Example 2: Pupil involvement in individual education plans at Cedar Hall

In the primary phase at Cedar Hall, teaching is predominantly class-based and pupils work with the same staff for most of each day. This teaching and learning regime means that individual education plans are seen as useful working documents to which both staff and pupils can frequently refer. This ease of access allows classroom staff, both teachers and support assistants, to work with pupils in order to review and update individual education plans regularly.

In the upper school at Cedar Hall, teaching is based on a mainstream secondary, subject-driven model. This means that an individual student may be taught by up to six teachers in any one day. Some members of staff may meet an individual student for only an hour or two each week. Under these circumstances, it is more difficult to coordinate the use of cross-curricular individual education plans. The task of maintaining individual education plans as working documents with relevance to day-to-day teaching and learning, and keeping associated records up to date across a range of subjects taught by a number of different members of staff, is inevitably complicated.

Staff decided that the students themselves could contribute to this situation in a positive way by taking responsibility for their own individual education plans. Each secondary age student at Cedar Hall is therefore given a flexible A5 sized ring-binder which acts as a diary or personal organiser. Individual students record their own key objectives for the term ahead in the ring-binder in the simple format provided (see Figure 2.5).

The objectives noted on these sheets are drawn from the priorities identified at each student's Annual Review, but students are encouraged to write them into their ring-binders using their own words. In accordance with the intentions of the *Programme of Action* (DfEE 1998), each objective may be broken down into no more than three targets, again in the students' own words.

Objective:	
Targets:	Review – comments and date:

Figure 2.5 Cedar Hall's format for recording against targets in students' personal organisers

In order to promote a further sense of ownership, students are encouraged to personalise their slimline folders with photographs, pictures or their own art work and to carry them around at all times. Giving students responsibility for maintaining their own individual education plans means that staff are no longer holding documents in easily forgotten or cumbersome files. Students themselves are encouraged to prompt their teachers to fill in the comments and review section and to sign off targets when they have been achieved. In the following examples (in Figure 2.6), drawn directly from the personal organisers carried by individual students in the upper school, pupils have:

- written their agreed objectives and related targets into the appropriate sections;
- prompted staff to record instances of achievement, with ticks, dates, initials and comments, in the review column. (Figure 2.6)

When targets are recorded as having been consistently achieved, students can negotiate a new set of targets, with reference again to the priorities identified at Annual Review, with their form tutor. Regular tutorials are now focused on individual education planning and on involving students in setting their own targets for learning. Since the beginnings of terms are always busy times in school, individual education plans are designed to run from half term to half term, with the cycle commencing in the term in which each student's Annual Review is held. Staff at Cedar Hall anticipate that giving students a significant degree of responsibility for their own individual education plans in this way will greatly enhance their involvement in the tutorial process and in the Annual Review itself.

Example 3: Case conferences at Longview Unit

In order to negotiate the content of individual education plans with pupils and students at Longview, a case conference is held once every six weeks for each young person. This meeting is attended by the core team (comprising all the Longview staff who work directly with the individual pupil or student); relevant professionals from outside the unit (staff from the mainstream school and the social worker, for example); the family; and the young person. The meeting is devoted to an evaluation of progress against the targets set for the previous six weeks. This evaluation in turn is based on a report which will have been written in the light of discussions with the young person concerned. The meeting then negotiates a revised set of targets for the six weeks ahead, with each pupil or student and members of their family being invited to add their comments. In this way, each individual education plan evolves from the baseline assessment process and is considered in the light of each young person's rate of progress. Liaison with the mainstream school, the family and, crucially, the young person is maintained throughout.

Objective: *To settle to work within five minutes*

Targets:	**Review – comments and date**
To sit down and get my things quickly	√ *HH* √ *M. Smith 11/10/99* √ *R. Jones 18/11/99* √ *M. Smith 18/11/99* √ *HH 26/11/99*

Objective: *Discussion skills*

Targets:	**Review – comments and date**
Be able to give a one minute account and opinion to class group	*1/2 √ HH 18/11/99*

Objective: *To use a dictionary*

Targets:	**Review – comments and date**
Find out the meanings of words I do not know in a dictionary	Found these words: bayonet, lark, squabble, brass and veil while in reading group M. Smith 24/11/99

Objective: *To be assertive*

Targets:	**Review – comments and date**
To be able to say NO in a big voice	C. Munro 20/11/99

Objective: *To improve punctuation*

Targets:	**Review – comments and date**
To use capital letters and full stops in all work	M. Smith 18/11/99 HH 22/11/99 √ M. Smith 23/11/99 C. Munro 24/11/99

Figure 2.6 Pupil-maintained individual education planning sheets from Cedar Hall School

Involving pupils in review and evaluation

Example 1: Annual Reviews at The Heath School

When the 'Involving Pupils' project began at The Heath School, pupils were not necessarily expected to attend their own Annual Review meetings. Pupils were invited and even encouraged to attend, but the final decision was left to them. Many pupils may have perceived the Annual Review meeting as just another forum in which their failures were highlighted, and were hesitant about attending. Whatever their reasons, they were often absent from important discussions concerning their own future prospects. As a result of the project, this situation was to change:

> *As a staff, we made a decision to change our expectations. All pupils now attend the review as a matter of right. There was some early pupil resistance to the concept but key staff involved with the pupils have spent time emphasising the importance of the meeting. Not only do the pupils now attend the review but as a consequence of the project copies of the annual review target are now available in all the personal record files for every pupil. These are a useful reminder and can be referred to quickly and easily. It is our aim for them to be part of the child's development throughout a year.*

In order to achieve this, staff at The Heath School developed an 'implementation review' process building on established practice. First, staff resolved to begin to hold meetings, involving the individual pupil, parents, school staff and possibly other professionals from outside agencies, six weeks after a pupil joins the school. The aims of this meeting are:

- to evaluate the pupil's initial period in school;
- to 'unpack' and then prioritise the pupil's targets for the forthcoming year.

The statement of special educational needs provides a reference point for discussions and the targets agreed at this meeting are subjected to scrutiny at Annual Review. The pupil's views are regarded as having a major contribution to make in helping the meeting to come to an understanding of the current situation and to establish a focus for the year ahead.

In order to monitor progress towards targets, form tutors and key workers developed what has come to be known as a 'round robin' recording sheet, which is circulated in order to gather information from all the staff concerned with a pupil. When information has been gathered from all relevant staff, form tutors or key workers meet with pupils individually in order to collate and evaluate the information. The prompt table provided here as Figure 2.7 is used to enable staff and pupils to work together in order to calculate an overall summary of progress towards each of the targets using the comments from a range of staff members. Using this format means that pupils are given the opportunity to evaluate the data for themselves in dialogue with a member of staff and to make a judgement about their own levels of success. It may then be possible for staff and pupils to discuss suggestions for new targets or areas of focus, if this is appropriate.

IEP Evaluation:

To be completed by Key Worker/Form Tutor and Pupil

Grade 1–5: 1: Excellent, 2: Very good, 3: Satisfactory, 4: A little progress, 5: No progress.

Target 1:

Target 2:

Target 3:

What Next ?

Figure 2.7 Evaluating progress towards targets at The Heath School

Example 2: Review and forward planning at Cedar Hall

All pupils at Cedar Hall have statements of special educational needs. On the occasion of the anniversary of each statement, parents and teaching staff, as well as any other relevant agencies, meet with the pupil in order to undertake an Annual Review of the pupil's progress against targets set the previous year. Prior to Cedar Hall joining the 'Involving Pupils' project, these Annual Review meetings were largely conducted in the absence of the pupil concerned. Unsurprisingly, the process and the outcomes had little meaning for pupils under these circumstances. The procedure now involves an informal one-to-one tutorial with the pupil before the Annual Review date using the schedule, adapted from Essex LEA Annual Review documentation, given as Figure 2.8. (A photocopiable version of this is available as Appendix 4, and a version adapted by The Edith Borthwick School using 'Widget' (the symbols programme), for use with pupils with communication difficulties as Appendix 5.)

Under this revised procedure, pupils are not only able to express their views in the tutorial held prior to the date of the Annual Review, but are usually involved in most, if not all, of the Annual Review meeting itself. Pupils have greeted this opportunity enthusiastically, as the following direct and incisive comment demonstrates:

At his most recent Annual Review, John, a usually quiet boy, took the adults by surprise. He was prepared to state quite plainly what the problems were that he was facing at school and how he should tackle them. When I asked him his views on whether pupils should be included in Annual Review meetings he subsequently said: 'Well, the meeting is about me so I should be in there.'

Pupils' views are taken into account when the upper school teaching and support staff discuss possible targets, both academic and social, a week before the review meeting. For example, it was widely felt among staff at Cedar Hall in 1997 that Anna, a girl then in Year 8, would benefit from part-time reintegration into

---

Annual Review – Pupil Views

This is a chance for you to say what you feel about your school and learning.
Please tell us as much as you can. An adult or friend can help you if you wish.

A: Last year at school
    What things did you most like doing?
    What did you do best?
    What improvements did you make?
    What helped you to learn or get on better?
    What things did you not like doing?
    What things did you find difficult?

B: Next year at school
    What things do you want to do better?
    What things do you need help with?
    Are you worried about anything?   If so, what?
    Would you like to talk to anyone else?   If so, who?

Signed: Helped by: Date:

Figure 2.8 Taking note of pupils' views at Cedar Hall School

mainstream school. These views were largely based on the academic progress that Anna had achieved. However, Anna clearly stated in her tutorial that she did not wish even to attempt reintegration at that stage. On reflection, staff decided that her low self-confidence and self-esteem had been overlooked. Anna's views were respected and the situation was reassessed. Targets were set with the aim of encouraging Anna to become more confident and independent. Among other things, she was given responsibility for helping with lower school swimming. A year later, with her self-esteem reinvigorated and with the benefit of seeing others in her year succeed in their reintegration placements, Anna became enthusiastic about the prospect of attempting reintegration in the immediate future.

Anna's story illustrates why staff at Cedar Hall have found that involving pupils in the decisions that affect their futures has to be wisely and gently handled. Many pupils arrive at the school from the mainstream of education having certainly experienced failure, and perhaps ridicule from their peers, because of their inability to fit in or cope. In the supportive atmosphere of Cedar Hall School most soon blossom and flourish, but some retain the fears and vulnerabilities associated with their mainstream experience. In the experience of staff at Cedar Hall, these anxieties do not simply disappear with the passage of time. The process of involving pupils therefore has to encompass more than simply encouraging pupils to be present at meetings concerning them or creating time and space for regular tutorial contact between staff and pupils. As the Cedar Hall report indicates, working with pupils who may have negative experiences of school can require staff to develop specialist skills:

A member of the support staff with whom pupils easily identify, has been given training in counselling and a timetable allocation to be available to listen to pupils and to provide support and advice. Pupils may refer themselves to her, or may be approached, having perhaps been pinpointed by other staff as someone who would benefit from counselling. We have found the words of Noonan (1990) to be true when she writes: 'Counselling works because it helps to reduce confusion . . . it turns the past into memories . . . frees us to have what is available in the present and makes us our own masters'.

Robert is an example of a child who has benefited from this input. He transferred from a local primary school into Year 7 at Cedar Hall. Robert had been coping with the academic challenge of mainstream education (in fact, he had an above-average reading age) but he appeared to have very low self-esteem and self-confidence. He initially presented as a very shy yet eloquent boy with mild cerebral palsy affecting his fine motor skills. He very soon became the most popular boy in his year group, however, because of his very mature and caring demeanour. His popularity may have helped his self-esteem, but it also meant that to some extent he was taken advantage of by one or two members of the class. It seemed that he was unable or unwilling to say 'no' to their constant attention-seeking.

Staff at Cedar Hall provided Robert with regular counselling, self-assertiveness training and opportunities to succeed. Gradually, over the subsequent two years, Robert's whole demeanour began to change and by the end of Year 8 it was gently suggested to him and his parents that he might benefit from part-time reintegration at a local mainstream school – something both he and his parents would at one time not have contemplated. After initial hesitation and with gentle encouragement, Robert agreed. The Cedar Hall report suggests that the availability of trusted members of staff and Robert's own involvement in the ongoing process of review and decision-making were crucial to the success of this initiative:

As the year has progressed, Robert's self-confidence has grown enormously. He and another boy from his year began by just spending one morning a week at the mainstream school, accompanied the whole time by a member of the Cedar Hall support staff. At the end of the term, Robert's views, and those of his teachers at the mainstream school, were asked for. His answer to the question: 'Would you like to spend more, less or the same amount of time at your new school?' surprised us. Robert said: 'More time because I love it.' His self-confidence clearly had developed beyond our expectations. His maths teacher at the school was also encouraging, stating that he was above the average for the set he was in.

The next step forward was to encourage Robert into attempting to stay at the mainstream school for the whole day, without adult support from Cedar Hall staff. Again in this he has not only coped but shone, and in asking for his opinions at the end of the spring term, Robert's response again showed a hunger for more time at the school.

Credit must be given to the mainstream school's special educational needs team, who have all the way been concerned to involve the pupils themselves in the decisions about their own future. At a recent review of the reintegration, now almost a year since its beginning for Robert, the special educational needs coordinator (SENCO) took the time to ensure that Robert's views were heard and, in response, has arranged for another day to be made available for reintegration involving some subjects of his choice. Surprising both the school and his parents, this choice included science, an area where previously Robert has felt unable to cope due to his difficulties in fine motor skill coordination. Perhaps this is another indicator of his improved self-confidence. Should this next step succeed, the possibility of a trial full-time reintegration might be considered.

The Cedar Hall School Counsellor has also recognised the changes in Robert and the important role played in his progress by the process of giving him a voice:

He's come on so much. His self-esteem has grown. Whereas when he started counselling he would not maintain eye contact and would sit hunched up, he now looks at you and sits in a relaxed manner. He would often perceive comments from others as criticism, which doesn't happen any more, and most importantly he will now attempt things he would not have done before.

Robert himself is also keenly aware of the benefits of becoming more actively involved in his own education. When asked why he thinks he is coping so well with the new challenges facing him at his new mainstream school, Robert said: 'It's because of the counselling and assertiveness training I have had.' Robert now recognises and articulates his own achievements. While travelling back to Cedar Hall from his mainstream placement in the minibus, after a lively discussion he remarked to the member of staff escorting him: 'Miss, a year ago I wouldn't have had the confidence to be speaking to you like this.' We offer an intriguing update on Robert's story in Chapter 5, 'Evaluation and Implications'.

Conclusions

Cedar Hall School

Pupil involvement in the process of individual education planning is now well established at Cedar Hall. Staff at Cedar Hall School summarise their revised approach to the Annual Review process in the flow chart given as Figure 2.9.

The targets mentioned in Figure 2.9 are those included in students' individual education plans. As we have noted above, students in the upper school at Cedar Hall are now responsible for overseeing the process of monitoring their own progress towards these targets.

A summary of the procedure for the Annual Review of pupil progress in the Upper school at Cedar Hall		
Time Scale	**Processes**	
At least 2 weeks before date of Annual Review:	Teaching Staff write pupil's report based on teacher assessments and send it to parents.	
	Parents fill in written questionnaire about their views on pupil's progress.	Form tutor holds tutorial with pupil.
Week before date of Annual Review:	Outside agencies meet with pupil and may write a report, e.g. educational psychologist and/or speech therapist.	Upper school staff meet to discuss and review pupil's progress and establish provisional targets for year ahead.
	At the Annual Review meeting, the form tutor and a member of the senior management team meet with the pupil and parents and relevant outside agencies (e.g. Educational Psychologist).	
In the week following Annual Review meeting:	Final targets fed back to upper school staff.	
Once a term:	Review of targets with pupil by form tutor.	

Figure 2.9 An overview of the Annual Review process in the upper school at Cedar Hall

Longview Unit

At all times, staff at the Longview Unit maintain the future educational needs of each young person under consideration. Through the multi-disciplinary case conferences, the various forms of reporting, the individual education plans themselves and the individual education plan review meetings, pupils and students are invited to share their perceptions with staff and to express their preferences with regard to future placements. Although pupils and students often return to the mainstream school they attended prior to admission to the Longview Unit, staff always regard the question of reintegration as an issue for negotiation. Discussions may focus, for example, on when and how reintegration is to be achieved. Sometimes pupils will request a change of school and Longview staff will become involved in exploring this possibility. Students in Year 11 may seek the support of Longview staff in considering and applying for placements directly into further education or alternative sixth form provision. In all these possible scenarios, the views and preferences of the young people themselves are sought, attended to and considered as central.

The Heath School

By the end of the 'Involving Pupils' project, targets had been set within individual education plans for every pupil at The Heath School for at least one term. Pupils in the pilot group had been involved in the cycle of target setting and review twice. Recording in relation to pupils' individual education plans has now also been integrated with the procedures for supporting pupils in managing their own behaviour at The Heath School. A 'points' system had been in use for some time prior to the 'Involving Pupils' project in order to help support and monitor behaviour management. Before the onset of the project, pupils could achieve two of the total of ten points for working hard in class or for behaving well or being supportive of staff or peers during 'out of class' time. Achievement in relation to individual education planning has now been incorporated into the system so that pupils who make progress towards their targets in a particular lesson or 'out of class' session may be rewarded with the two bonus points. A further innovation has involved displaying a record of all the pupils' 'out of class' targets in year group order in the school file room. This display serves to remind staff about individual pupil's targets and is particularly important when it comes to rewarding points for the 'out of class' sessions in the school day.

A summary of the various stages of the project at The Heath School is given as Figure 2.10. The Heath School proforma for IEP action planning is shown as Appendix 6, along with completed examples showing one pupil's progress over a six month period.

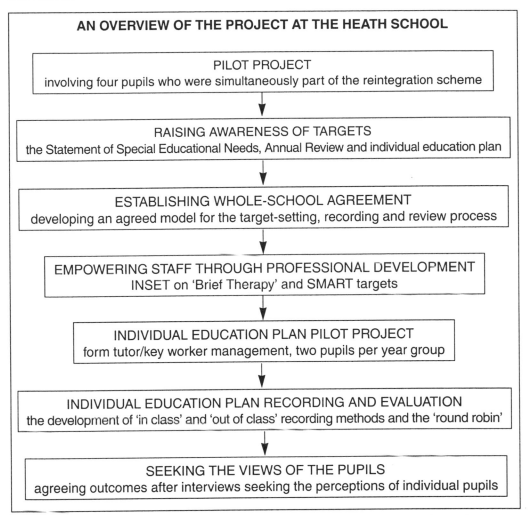

Figure 2.10 An overview of the 'Involving Pupils' project at The Heath School

CHAPTER 3

The Practice – Teaching thinking skills

This chapter follows the work of participating schools in introducing and developing thinking skills programmes in order to give students greater control over their own learning. This work formed a rich vein throughout the project, supported by some of the leading writers on, and exponents of, thinking skills whose contributions will be referred to during this section. A variety of thinking skills programmes are referred to by title (in italics) during this section. Full references to these materials can be found in the 'Resources' section.

Introduction

> I am very impressed by the growing evidence of the impact on standards of systematic teaching of thinking skills. This is not about some loosely defined or woolly approach to study skills. It is about the ability to analyse and make connections, to use knowledge effectively, to solve problems and to think creatively. It is about developing mental strategies to take on both academic and wider challenges.
>
> (David Blunkett, Education and Employment Secretary, January 2000)

The powerful movement of thinking skills in the latter half of the twentieth century, heavily inspired by the work of Reuven Feuerstein with stateless and culturally deprived young people in Israel after the holocaust, has influenced many schools, while providing, still, insubstantial research evidence on how the teaching of thinking skills impacts on pupil autonomy. Feuerstein developed and pioneered the structured thinking skills programme *Instrumental Enrichment* (IE) over 40 years ago.

Savell *et al.* (1986) reported on the effects of recent trials of the IE programme in Canada, Israel, US and Venezuela, concluding that the impact of IE training was most evident in the area of non-verbal measures of intelligence (figurative and spatial information), while impact (although difficult to interpret) had also been made on:

- student self-esteem;
- improved behaviour in classrooms;
- better performance on attainment and achievement tests.

More recently Dr Branco Weiss and Israel's then Minister of Education, Culture and Sports, established in 1990 the Branco Weiss Institute, the 'School for Teaching Thinking' in Jerusalem and the 'Wide Angle' Teachers Center in the north of Israel. Many leading exponents of thinking skills have also emerged in the United States, Canada and Britain, some of whom have been involved with the work of schools in this section of the book.

The concept of *empowerment* and *autonomy for learners* through the teaching of thinking skills (Gardner 1993, de Bono 1993, Sharron 1994) is central to the development of a curriculum which is meaningful and provides knowledge and understanding relevant to people's life experiences. The arrival in schools of the revised *National Curriculum for England* (DfEE/QCA 1999) serves only to emphasise the continuing prescriptive nature of curriculum structure as we move into the new millennium. There is still neither time nor space to include programmes of learning into our curriculum which deal with the essence of *how to learn*. The real challenge for teachers is to discover how to match the preferred learning styles and needs of individuals to the curriculum structure. Arguably, teaching pupils how to *think* can lead to pupils thinking how to *learn* – becoming more autonomous and gaining control over their own learning. The DfEE have acknowledged this, and in October 1998 commissioned Carol McGuinness of Queens University, Belfast, to review and evaluate research into thinking skills. McGuinness (1999) asserts that, in order to respond to the challenges of the new century, people must be empowered, autonomous and able to 'take charge of their own learning'.

The work of schools on thinking skills within this project is illuminating and provides illustrations of the potency of the application of the various materials and programmes described. Although no generalisations can be made as to the long-term effect of thinking skills teaching, it is clear that student outcomes are positive and, in some cases, students are able to express for themselves what a difference working on thinking skills has made to them.

Four schools focused on the teaching of thinking skills as a major element of their work in the project. Each provision approached the teaching of thinking skills from a different starting point:

In Market Field School it was envisaged that, by developing the thinking and language skills of the targeted group, students would then have better access to other curriculum areas, would extend their ability to think creatively and would begin to develop a systematic approach to problem-solving.

Priory School focused on development of the teaching of thinking skills as part of the personal and social education curriculum and syllabus for pupils in Years 7 to 11. The school was concerned with considering alternative teaching and learning approaches and materials to help students have more positive learning experiences, promote relationships and teamwork, and celebrate achievements. Thinking skills materials were introduced to pupil groups and the effectiveness of their use tracked and evaluated using mainly video evidence of teaching and learning sessions.

In Longview Unit the starting points were:

- the wish to reconsider curricular organisation and provision in order to respond to the changing needs of young persons admitted to the Unit;
- to develop an outreach service post-discharge to offer support to schools.

Reasons for these starting points related to:

- the changing nature of illness being addressed, e.g. psychosis, severe eating disorders, clinical depression and severe self harm/suicidal tendencies, all of which have a major effect on an individual's cognitive functioning, capacity to make and sustain relationships and work in a group context: young people at Longview will continue to experience many of these difficulties post-discharge and so full-time reintegration to mainstream schools is problematic;
- the pressures of the National Curriculum and examination course work which make prolonged absence in Years 10 and 11 a major issue, especially when considering reintegration;
- the overriding need for disadvantaged/disaffected/vulnerable young people to be empowered to take hold of learning again for themselves, developing skills that will be relevant and purposeful to them in the future;
- the willingness, or otherwise, of schools to work effectively with young people post-discharge.

These issues were addressed through the development of a thinking skills programme and the development of an outreach service.

The Edith Borthwick School started with the premise that, in order to process and present information and knowledge effectively, pupils and students have to think and reason. The school attempted to address this area by piloting the teaching of thinking skills as a discrete subject area.

These starting points can be summarised in three major strands – teaching thinking skills:

- *as an entitlement within the whole curriculum*, where pupils are taught the strategies of thinking either discretely or through other subjects;
- *as a means of access to other subjects and areas of learning*, where pupils are able to generalise their thinking skill strategies into other subject areas and to other learning situations;
- *as a route to reintegration and inclusion*, where the acquisition of thinking skills and study skills enable pupils to integrate more successfully into other provision, especially mainstream schools.

The projects undertaken in each provision are now described under the above headings.

Thinking skills as an entitlement within the whole curriculum

Example 1: Processing and presenting information, knowledge, and ideas to others: The Edith Borthwick School

The notion of flexible learning was examined through a number of initiatives based on student views and perceptions regarding their preferred learning styles. This led to an understanding of the main skill areas necessary for students to access learning across the whole curriculum. These are summarised as:

- identify and isolate problems
- organise/structure thoughts
- arrive at feasible solutions
- make informed decisions/judgements
- assess consequences of actions to self and others
- respect and consider the alternative view/need
- introduce the basic elements of discussion and debate.

Two members of teaching staff attended a three-day interactive course run by Frances Link, an international thinking skills trainer. The course involved participants as receivers and experimenters in thinking skills exercises and programmes. It also taught participants how to approach organising the teaching of thinking skills as a discrete lesson on a regular basis.

A one year programme was initially based around a selection of ideas and approaches put forward by Frances Link. A further selection of teaching materials was adapted from:

- *Thinking to Write* – Frances Link
- *Pupil Profiles of Cognitive Development*
- *Think Talk Connect Activities* – Robert Wirtz
- *CoRT Thinking Skills* – Edward de Bono
- *Creative Thinking* – Stick Picture Drawings – Andrew Wright
- *Pictures from Sound* – Listening and Thinking/Looking and Thinking
- *Somerset Thinking Skills Course*
- *On the Track Problem Solving*
- *Instrumental Enrichment* – Reuven Feuerstein.

A variety of approaches were used to teach thinking skills. These included whole-class discussion (brainstorming), circle-time sessions based on the work of Jenny Mosley (see *Quality Circle Time* in the 'Resources' section), individual task setting (especially when developing spatial awareness), paired activity games. Some of the materials in *Somerset Thinking Skills*, *Top Ten Thinking Tactics* and *Instrumental*

Enrichment (through an IE trained teacher) were delivered using the above styles. Teachers noticed that the group, over a period of time, became used to the routine of:

- listening to initial instructions;
- looking at the resource sheet silently;
- answering focused questions through turn-taking;
- gathering possible solutions;
- trialling solutions individually, in pairs, small groups or whole classes;
- finding consensus.

This type of routine is described as 'really useful' by one of the students, Sam, in the pilot group who later became fully integrated into a secondary mainstream school. The Edith Borthwick report includes a transcript of Sam's view of how thinking skills helped him understand his own ability to 'bridge' between subjects of the curriculum:

> *I was taught by two teachers doing thinking skills. One of them used to talk through the lesson while the other one helped us. Then they swapped over, so you had to get used to listening to each one. It was hard cos they had different ways of doing it and when 'sir' did it, it was slow and when 'miss' did it, she did it fast and it was hard to catch up. But you wanted to, so you thought hard . . . you listened hard, you know, got your head down and it was good. You felt good, everyone felt good cos you always found an answer.*

> *Then, when they showed you what you'd done, I saw it was like a pattern . . . like, you get the instructions, you know, the task; then you set down the problem so you can see it . . . I mean, you can draw it if you want. Then you work out how you could solve it, then you try it out. If you get the solution you can share it, if somebody else does they can . . . if you both get a solution you can decide on the best one. But you can all do it.*

> *Then I thought, well, when I was in maths, that's how I'd do it. I'd do 'listen, draw the problem, think the way to work it out, try it out, check if it's right'. It works, you know. It even works in history, like when they ask you how many wives Henry had and you don't know, so you set it down and I drew a picture of a book about history. Then I asked about where to get it. When I got it, it was simple. You just need the tools.*

This is an example of a student finding his way through the complex nature of 'how we learn'. Sam knew that he had found a new way of helping himself to find answers and became more and more confident in receiving instructions in all subject areas, understanding the task, finding ways to reach a solution and getting there.

Consistently good results came from keeping theory to a minimum, and creating a practical activity in learning situations where clear achievable objectives were set.

Suitable challenges in design and technology have been: Build a ten second timer for a marble run; Use construction equipment to build a house for a hamster. During these challenges pupils practised the skills of receiving and processing information, considering the problem, analysing the problem, considering solutions, testing solutions and finding solutions. This is the same pattern that Sam described above. Also, at least one of the same staff were involved, due to the arrangements made by the school for team-teaching to take place in key subjects during the project. Practical problems encountered in making the items were explored by the use of small groups and direct questioning. Pupils would signal when they were stuck. Staff would mediate by leading pupils through a series of questions which verified what they had done so far, by enabling them to express the exact problem by reflecting back their actions, and by prompting a series of possible solutions to the problem, until pupils took over again and made their choices. This type of 'mediation' is consistent with the approaches of trainers in *Instrumental Enrichment* (See 'Resources' section).

Therefore, some team teaching staff working within Key Stage 3 were able to focus directly on the presenting factors which are inhibiting the development of social and academic skills. It was a slow process, but clear benefits have been seen in the development of social skills, turn-taking, listening, teamwork, self-confidence. During the life of the project thinking skills were targeted in IEPs. The pilot group of 14 students began with two targets each. By the end of term one none of the targets had been fully met. By the end of term two 20 out of 28 targets had been met. By the end of the third term all 28 targets had been demonstrated and 18 new targets met. Although no generalisations can be made from these figures, it is clear that all students in this group were able to meet targets successfully through the use of thinking skills systems. Practical-based activities utilising the subject areas of drama, English, personal, social and health education, mathematics, art, history, information and communication technology and design technology have all been used to promote thinking skills.

The pilot has revealed some indicators which have been acknowledged within the ongoing development of thinking skills programmes:

- Students have great difficulties in analysing problems and presenting a variety of solutions or factors to prioritise.
- The urge to create or solve a problem quickly often overcomes the thought processes involved in planning, selecting, and rejecting.
- Thinking skills do not lend themselves to being taught in isolation.
- The acquired skills and strategies need a real context for practise across the curriculum.
- Students often exhibit poorly developed listening skills and associated difficulties in processing of speech.
- Students often experience difficulty in accepting others' viewpoints, or the alternative view.

As a result, there remains a very real dilemma for teaching staff. They have recognised that their emphasis in teaching is on the verbal instruction route. They acknowledge that they have often failed to appreciate that the majority of students are not sufficiently skilled in listening and processing speech to understand the content of teaching. This is one of the factors leading to the school developing a 'Total Communication' policy (described later in this section and presented in full as Appendix 7).

The future development of thinking skills is being directed through a curriculum subject-based approach including: design technology, English, mathematics, drama, science, art and personal, social and health education. In addition to this there will be discrete thinking skills 'top up' activities using elements from the *Instrumental Enrichment, Think Talk Connect,* Think to Write, Creative Thinking, and *Top Ten Thinking Tactics* programmes.

The application and teaching of thinking skills will take on a more cross-curricular or subject-context dimension, each task having an attainable objective which is more easily identified by the student and recorded as a priority on his or her IEP.

Although students experience difficulty in developing their thinking skills, they certainly relish the challenge and few give up. Progress has certainly been made with the pilot group. The further development of such skills is of critical importance as they enable access across the curriculum. When reminded, students within the pilot group are now able to stop, think, plan, and select appropriate methods and materials. This has largely been achieved on an individual basis. Two students have used their developing skills in full and have been fully reintegrated into mainstream schools.

The next challenge is to extend the individual progression to a small group or whole-class context. Until social skills are further developed from joint problem-solving activities, students will not have sufficient experience to debate and evaluate other opinions, select and reject ideas, and work on common strategies.

Example 2: Teaching thinking skills to access the whole curriculum and beyond: Longview Unit

The following commentary was written by teachers developing thinking skills materials and approaches in the Unit:

Instead of focusing on the curriculum, we wanted to concentrate on the individual young person's ability to develop cognitive key skills and strategies that would most effectively benefit them whatever they moved on to. In other words, rather than continuing to focus specifically on the curriculum as per mainstream schools, we now wanted to pursue the idea of enabling young persons to handle unfamiliar problems and learning tasks independently. As stated in the Elton report, 'Pupils are not passive receivers of education. They have to participate in their learning . . .' (DES 1989). Specifically we wanted each young person to gain an understanding of, and a belief in, their ability to change and develop their thinking and learning skills. Whilst continuing to use the mainstream curriculum as the basic structure, our focus would change to identifying the factors that inhibit the individual pupil from learning and then helping that pupil to be aware of those difficulties and develop skills and strategies to improve them. This would be reflected across the total curriculum but would have its hub as an hourly thinking skills session each week.

We began by developing the latter.

Having researched various programmes through articles, books, observation and discussion we decided to trial a thinking skills programme called Top Ten Thinking Tactics. *This is based on Feuerstein's work as outlined by Sharron (1994).*

Essentially Feuerstein argues that every child can be changed by education and that intellectual skills can be taught. Instead of accepting children as they are, Feuerstein's aim is to deliberately transform children's development. This philosophy seemed to coincide very closely with our own and we therefore decided to pursue it further.

Top Ten Thinking Tactics *was well received by the young people involved. Comments on the individual evaluation sheets included:*

'I never realised how I actually used [thinking skills] everyday. It surprised me!'

'It can give you confidence to realise that you **can** *change things: they don't have to stay the way they are.'*

'[Thinking skills] seem to happen naturally, but you could work on all of them.'

Teacher group evaluation led mainly to a recognition of the varying levels of work that we achieve whilst seemingly 'just teaching the curriculum'. Specifically that our academic input is built upon the therapeutic foundations of raising self-esteem, restoring self-confidence, enabling the young person to recognise and acknowledge their strengths and achievements and on developing problem solving skills.

Teacher feedback also included such comments as:

'Very structured, with clearly defined skill areas.'

'Material can be differentiated to meet all ability levels but it essentially remains very young, possibly a disadvantage with our young persons.'

This programme was indeed designed for junior aged pupils so we decided to explore Reuven Feuerstein's Instrumental Enrichment *work further through other sources.*

Augustine Filson from the Sankofa Institute, London, visited to explain the work of his establishment. It has committed itself to Feuerstein's approach, involving the Learning Potential Assessment Device *(LPAD) designed to assess a student's potential to learn and* Instrumental Enrichment *(IE) programmes designed to build up thinking and learning skills by way of a carefully graded cognitive programme; both of these then bridged to a full social and educational curriculum, and an environment directed to rebuilding pupils' personal and cultural identities.*

Whilst this seemed to reflect much of our emphasis within the Unit classroom, it also needed to be intensive and long term and therefore not conducive to the flexibility required in the multi-disciplinary setting nor to the average length of stay. Training costs were also well outside our budget. After staff discussion we decided that, whilst this programme was admirable and seemingly effective, it was not practicable for us.

They turned to the *Somerset Thinking Skills Course* (STSC), also based on Feuerstein's work, and invited Nigel Blagg, it's co-writer and exponent, to run a workshop for all interested schools involved in the project.

This scheme seemed much more applicable to the setting. It was designed to be used in schools, and while focusing on the core essence of transforming children's thinking did not require a total commitment. It was also adaptable, so that staff were able to devise a thinking skills programme of their own based on STSC that would be appropriate to short-term programmes of treatment (average six months). This consisted of 12-week blocks focusing on:

- ways of approaching a task
- pinpointing the problem
- organising thoughts
- changing strategy
- spatial awareness
- temporal awareness
- consequences of actions
- clear communication
- listening skills
- deduction
- memory.

At this stage two members of staff took on specific responsibility for developing the thinking skills policy and associated schemes of work. Following a trial of two blocks, young people and staff were asked for their thoughts on the effectiveness of this programme. Staff comments were:

There are difficulties with the wide range of abilities and mental illness that we meet within the Unit group.

It is a useful group process.

There are good opportunities for observations of young people in a group setting.

We need to look at how we record areas of difficulty and incorporate them into their individual programmes.

We are beginning to look more closely at teaching styles and approaches across the curriculum in relation to empowering young people.

Due to varying lengths of stay, some young people are at risk of covering the same programmes again.

It's sometimes difficult to know what the main focus of the session is.

Young people's comments were mixed. Many were in need of help in seeing the relevance of thinking skills to all areas of their lives. Some benefits were noted by individuals, particularly in relation to improved communication skills.

When compared to the evaluations on the *Top Ten Thinking Tactics* it seemed that the more specifically focused sessions were the most effective. Certainly young people found one target more useful, particularly in relation to applying that skill to other areas of their lives.

Another scheme was therefore brought into the thinking skills programme, *Skills for Adolescence* (see 'Resources' section). The aim of this scheme is to help young people learn how to deal with the challenges of a complex society by offering positive growth experiences and teaching specific coping skills. The course focuses on such themes as:

- building self-confidence through better communication
- improving peer relationships
- developing critical thinking skills for decision-making
- developing competence through better communication.

Initially this was trialled as a 12-week block in its own right and evaluation comments included:

I found the Skills for Adolescence *programmes useful. It related more to me and was more focussed, so was easier.*

I've learnt a lot about myself. The success line was really good as it pulled my life together as a whole and made it seem bigger and better. Suddenly it wasn't as bad as it had seemed!

I particularly liked the teamwork things, like strategies and comparisons. We did an exercise on building cube blocks and our team won because we had worked together and planned a strategy. The other team had all worked on their own, so we looked at comparisons between the two styles.

I thought the three-legged stool was the most helpful because I was able to list positive things about myself that I had never been able to do before.

The only session I found useful was the three-legged stool as we pointed out positive things about ourselves which I have found difficult in the past.

I didn't find any session useful.

Again, evaluation suggested the more specifically focused sessions to be the most useful. Following this trial a Unit Policy for Thinking Skills was developed with schemes of work which incorporated elements from the three programmes trialled.

Example 3: Beginning with the personal and social education curriculum: Priory School

At Priory School the teaching of thinking skills was introduced to pupils from Years 7 to 11. The premise was that personal and social education is a cross-curricular element, teaching skills and attitudes that would enable pupils with emotional and behavioural difficulties to grow in self-esteem and recognise their own power to exercise and control change. This sense of personal values permeated the approach to thinking skills, offering pupils opportunities to:

- assist and promote divergent thinking processes;
- demonstrate alternative strategies for learning;
- clarify and/or simplify complex issues, such as relationships, prioritising, and self-awareness;
- offer a 'change' of learning style and content, in order to sustain concentration within a structured lesson;
- encourage pupils' thinking and subsequent involvement in lessons;
- promote self-confidence through effective participation;
- ensure that pupils experience success and achievement;
- promote speaking and listening skills involving cross-curricular evaluation with the English department and English GCSE;
- promote and encourage effective group work;
- develop an 'appetite' for learning.

At present, the materials used in this connection are based on the *Somerset Thinking Skills Course, Top Ten Thinking Tactics*, and *Looking and Thinking*. Materials are selected from these sources and utilised in accordance with the age and maturity of the pupils, and the personal and social education topic being studied at the time.

In order to investigate the teaching of thinking skills and the impact on individual pupils, three sample exercises were used, being taken from Module 1 of the *Somerset Thinking Skills Course*, described below:

Number 4 – An 'abstract' exercise where pupils have to use dots, stars or intersections to locate the corners of a triangle and a square in 16 separate frames.

Number 9 – An 'open ended' exercise where pupils look at a drawing of a woman lost in a featureless landscape and have to use picture clues to explore how she might work her way out of the situation.

Number 19 – A 'search' exercise where pupils study a drawing of a bedroom scene with a number of clues about what might have happened in the scene.

In each case, the exercises were presented in the usual style of teaching and learning, and the group of pupils were filmed working. On the following day, pupils were debriefed individually via a discussion and evaluation sheet. The groups were also shown a playback of the filmed lesson. The essential input by the teacher was mediation. The object of the approach was to illustrate how successful the teaching of thinking skills is with regard to promoting collaborative and cooperative learning through group work with pupils with emotional and behavioural difficulties.

One of the videos shows a Year 9 group taking part in the lesson. There are seven pupils sitting around a table. The teacher sits outside the group and gives instructions and directs the group. At one stage he intervenes and stops the lesson as pupils are off task, beginning to distract one another and clearly not able to work as a group. Petty bickering ensues, with pupils making negative comments about the materials, the lesson and each other. Video footage shot several weeks later shows the same group enter the room, using the same places, and begin the task at hand (number 19 above). It is five minutes before the teacher makes a comment: 'What are the boxes at the bottom for?' The pupils almost ignore him, but not, this time, because they are disaffected. It seems like a completely different group. There is structure, there are rules, created and maintained by the seven pupils. The attitudes and atmosphere are positive, pupils work effectively towards a solution and are keen to explain to their teacher how and why they got there. The teacher explains:

It is incredible to watch. When you compare their starting points to what they achieved in six weeks of working, it's amazing! The pupils are very different. They have learnt to cooperate because they got hooked on the challenge. They wanted to find solutions and they were willing to go through the process together. If we could apply this to all subjects in the curriculum we really would be making progress! I really became a 'mediator' for the group. They would only use me if they needed to check something, find more information or confirm whether or not it was a good decision.

Priory School made progress with all teaching groups from Year 7 to 11. They used a mixed cocktail of materials, but with a systematic approach to teaching. Encouraged by their results they began to question how impact could be made into other curriculum areas.

Thinking skills as a means of access to other subjects and areas of learning

Example 1: Top Ten Thinking Tactics *and history – Market Field School*

Market Field School trialled the *Top Ten Thinking Tactics*, used with a group of Year 8 students for developing thinking and language skills, which would give them better access to the other curriculum areas, would extend their ability to think creatively and would begin to develop a systematic approach to problem-solving. The group was made up of four boys and four girls with a range of learning difficulties, behavioural difficulties and physical disabilities. One of the girls has severe speech impairment and one of the boys no expressive language, communicating mainly by Lightwriter. Two of the group are relatively articulate and several members of the group have good general knowledge. Literacy and numeracy skills are generally underdeveloped. Members of the group have differing social skills which range from extreme shyness to habitual attention-seeking behaviour.

A 30-minute session was allocated, led by one of the contributors with the other recording the session on video or making written notes. The following commentary describes the process:

In the first session the students were introduced to the Pupils Sheet with a focus on the first four items:

- *pinpointing the problem*
- *systematic search*
- *planning*
- *correct communication.*

A considerable amount of explanation of the four tactics was necessary and the conventions of discussion were agreed (e.g. listening to other people's opinions, giving equal value to opinions, being allowed to disagree).

Activity 1 – Getting the Right Order (see Appendix 8) was introduced and Part A was used as an example to illustrate how the first four tactics could be applied.

After this first session it was decided to set up an additional indicator of the use of thinking and language skills that would be linked to a specific subject area (history). This would take the form of two debates, one at the beginning of term and one towards the end after several sessions of the Top Ten Tactics.

The first debate would centre on the trial of Charles I in 1649. The group had been studying the Civil War as a unit of the Key Stage 3 history curriculum and the teacher/contributor gave them a description of the personalities and beliefs of each of the following: Archbishop Laud, a Cornish peasant, Henry Ireton, John Pym, Prince Rupert, Oliver Cromwell, Charles I. There would also be three judges.

It was necessary for the teacher to guide the choice of character made by each student because of the varying complexities of each part to be played. Students were also given a simple script to work from and/or use as a prompt. The three students who have greatest difficulty with expressive language were chosen to be the three judges, in order to ensure that they were active participants in the trial.

The second debate would be a 'balloon debate' and the students would be given the opportunity to choose their own character from past or present. This would follow on from Activity 5 of the Top Ten Tactics (see Appendix 9) which was felt to be a passive exercise that would lead into the debate and pupils would become more involved if they were given the opportunity to be 'real' people. The characters were chosen as follows: Queen Elizabeth I, Henry Ford, Queen Elizabeth II, Diana, Princess of

Wales, Roger Bacon, Oliver Cromwell, Rolf Harris, Florence Nightingale.

The characters would be required to justify their own survival and to vote on who should be thrown out of the balloon. They would be asked to give reasons for their choices.

Over the next 14 weeks the group worked on the materials in sequential order. During the third week the trial of Charles I took place and in the last week the balloon debate took place.

The students were enthusiastic from the outset but initial sessions were heavily teacher-led. Care was taken that all members of the group felt secure and all were encouraged to take part in the discussions. The two most confident and dominant members of the group were encouraged to let others contribute according to the agreed conventions. Initially, discussion was mainly between teacher and student and not student with student. All members of the group listened well. The use of the video recorder was inhibiting at first.

Teacher comments throughout the module were recorded, indicating students becoming more relaxed and familiar with the materials as the weeks progressed, showing increased understanding of the process. The following description of the last activity and balloon debate typifies the range of responses generated from students and the questions raised for teachers.

Activity 5 was then introduced as a precursor to the balloon debate. It took an unexpected amount of time for the students to demonstrate an understanding of what was happening in the picture. For example, the helicopter was not immediately identified as a rescue helicopter; the woman in the boat was said to look relaxed and the lightning was not identified as such. The relationship between the words beneath the picture and the picture itself had to be pointed out . . . The activity showed that only Grant had fixed ideas about the value of people's lives. Many of the group appeared bewildered by some of the ideas expressed and by the actual activity. Kay and Anna were willing to voice their opinions but showed no great depth of thought – just 'gut feelings' about people. The main difficulty seemed to be the students' inability to imagine the situation in the picture and then make judgements.

This activity was followed in the next session by the balloon debate. Having chosen their characters students had been asked to research them and develop their own speech from what they had found out. Whereas in the previous task (boat) they were commenting as onlookers, in the debate they had to role-play their chosen character and understand the arguments of the others. Students enjoyed the debate. Anna was concentrating really well and giving much more thought to her reasoning than before. However, it was quickly apparent that students were choosing the person they wanted to be thrown overboard based on their relationship with the student playing the role (i.e. part of the usual group dynamics). When asked to give reasons for their choices they came up with reasons related to the character they were playing rather than the person. For example, Steven chose Henry Ford because he wanted Grant to be out of the debate but when asked to give a reason he said that 'his cars were too expensive'.

Both these activities demonstrated students' difficulties with creative thinking and role play. The first activity showed that students have great difficulty in picking up the visual clues from the picture. However, all the students seemed to be more involved in the discussion and were much more comfortable with following the conventions of discussion (e.g. much improved listening skills were demonstrated).

There are clearly a number of factors which influence the success of the type of programme illustrated above. These include:

- the range of individual needs of the teaching group;
- the range of teaching and learning styles they are used to;
- student readiness to take on change – the culture of teaching and learning in the school;
- the need for materials to be differentiated at every level – particularly by outcome;
- teacher/learning support assistant skills in teaching and supporting communication.

Example 2: Links and bridges to mainstream – Longview Unit

Longview gathered valuable feedback from students relating to access to the wider curriculum and to reintegration into mainstream schools. It was clear that, once students had become used to the range of strategies and approaches to problem-solving taught through thinking skills, they could see ways of generalising those skills to their wider lives.

Monitoring and evaluation was addressed by weekly entries in the record sheets of young persons' Record of Achievement folders, which recorded how well the young person used the session and whether any particular difficulties had been experienced.

Student evaluations took place through group discussions and individual interview. The following comments were made:

I have developed some problem-solving skills and learnt strategies to use them. There are several different ways to solve problems like talking about and sharing ideas, building up slowly, tackling a bit at a time and to keep on trying until the problem is solved.

The opportunity to think around why things may have happened and what could have been done differently.

I didn't find the two sessions I went to useful.

There were boring bits like 'using figures of speech' and 'coded conversation'. I didn't see the point of them so didn't see how they were going to help.

The deduction ones were best.

I didn't really know what the sessions were about, but I was willing to give them a go to find out.

What I am taking away with me from these programmes is the confidence to speak out and say clearly what I really think. This has particularly helped to get me back to school.

Some of the messages above are powerful and illustrate the increased confidence shown by many students. The need for personal survival strategies is seen clearly by students. The emphasis given to these 'access to learning' skills for disaffected students in the mainstream curriculum is significantly underdeveloped.

Example 3: Processing and presenting information, knowledge, and ideas to others – The Edith Borthwick School

Within the research carried out by The Edith Borthwick School, major emphasis was placed on flexible learning styles and strategies. It was recognised that pupils will gain stronger access to a wider curriculum if they have acquired some of the skills of receiving, processing and outputting information.

In order to process and present information and knowledge effectively, pupils and students have to think and reason. The school has attempted to address this area by piloting the teaching of thinking skills as a discrete subject area, described earlier in this section.

The Edith Borthwick School has extended the approach to thinking skills as a part of whole-curriculum planning. Staff meetings were held to discuss the outcomes of the project work, with individual project workers giving a presentation of progress and outcomes. The links between thinking skills and communication, individual target setting and teaching and learning styles were established during these meetings, feeding into a management review of the school development plan. Within the revised school development plan, the following points of focus have emerged from the thinking skills pilot.

1. Production of a total communication policy, which outlines and develops the range of ways in which students can increase their communication. The 'Statement of Intent' reads:

    We intend to empower pupils and students through communication in order to give them increased self-esteem, confidence, competence, independence, ability to make and sustain relationships and participation in informed decision-making leading to more control over their own lives.

    To achieve this we intend to develop all the strands of total communication:

    Total Communication *is understood to mean the way in which people make their needs, desires, personal preferences and feelings known to other people through:*

- *speech*
- *reading, writing, using symbols*
- *gesture and signing*
- *facial expressions*
- *body language*
- *touch*
- *voice features (vocalisation)*

and through the use of:

- *listening skills*
- *social skills, including mirroring, turn-taking*
- *response and understanding*
- *touching and leading*
- *visual and written prompts, including objects of reference*
- *eye contact and other modes of physical and facial expression*
- *signing systems (e.g. Makaton)*
- *symbol systems (e.g. Writing with Symbols)*
- *social use of language*
- *information and communication technology*
- *alternative and augmentative communication (e.g. touchtalkers, liberators, communication boards, visual 'passports')*

and organise them into a 'common language' in order to select the most appropriate modes of communication to meet individual needs.

(The full policy is presented as Appendix 7.)

2. The planning of thinking/problem-solving targets in all individual education plans (IEPs). Each pupil/student now has a set of priority targets on the front cover of the IEP, covering English and communication, maths, information and communication technology, thinking or problem-solving skills.
3. The development of teaching and learning styles which focus on problem-solving, initially through English, maths, science, art, design technology, drama, personal, social and health education. Staff will be either team-teaching or working with small groups of students to pilot new approaches to delivering these subjects.

Thinking skills as a route to integration and inclusion

Example 1: Longview Unit

Longview Unit made specific reference to the issues of reintegrating/including students who have been accessing specialist provision into the mainstream. Emerging from student views and reflections was a strong view that the thinking skills approach had led to higher levels of self-confidence and self-esteem:

Without doubt our present programme offers broader experiences and opportunities than our original provision, particularly in relation to developing skills and strategies that would most effectively benefit them in the future. Feedback has shown that young people have gained an understanding of, and a belief in, their ability to change and develop their thinking and learning skills.

Our whole programme focuses on raising self-esteem and self-confidence and so it is not appropriate to attribute this specifically to the work involved in this project. However, once again feedback suggests that particular elements of the programme have specifically contributed to increased self-confidence particularly in relation to school reintegration.

Impact on the curriculum

Before recognising the need for change in the light of present admissions, Longview's curriculum was completely led by each young person's mainstream school. Staff have now embarked on a complete revision of their curriculum provision and are in the process of drawing up schemes of work for all subject areas so that they can more effectively meet the needs of all young people whatever their circumstances.

They have also extended the range of their curricular provision by introducing a variety of schemes that reflect the new emphasis on enabling and empowering. Some of their examples follow.

- *Successmaker: an integrated learning system, which enables young persons to work on improving their numeracy and literacy skills. It provides an individual course mapped to each student's needs resulting in significant learning gains as well as identifying specific and individual areas of need for teacher intervention. Youngsters work on their own on the computer, recording their results and receiving regular feedback from the teacher on their progress. It seems to be a motivating and stimulating programme.*
- *ASDAN Youth Award Scheme: an accredited award system which encourages independent learning and development of key skills. It is self-directed and involves the setting of targets and reviewing of work achieved. (ASDAN: The Key Skills Qualification (available from September 2000) recognises achievement in the key skills of communication, application of number and IT.)*
- *Examination opportunities: we have been successfully offering RSA core text processing and word processing qualifications for some time now, but have recently added RSA, CLAIT and the AEB 'On demand' tests in numeracy and literacy to our list of opportunities.*
- *IEPs: these now include an increasing number of targets specifically related to thinking skills and problem-solving.*

These developments have themselves been monitored regularly with the young people. One of Longview staff's concerns centred on the young people who need to maintain a heavy workload because of realistic GCSE commitments. Would the introduction of these alternative schemes seriously impact on their ability to keep up with the necessary schoolwork? Feedback from individual interviews included:

There seems to be the right sort of balance. Actually doing something else is a welcome break and enables me to get on better with my school work when I get back to it.

None of it is obligatory. I felt I could concentrate on my school work if I needed to.

Overall I think the programmes did help me to think more logically.

Our improved assessments are now related to the thinking skills targets and, as ASDAN is developed, will be linked with the key skills.

Longview Unit are also considering the difficulties faced by mainstream schools in including students from alternative or specialist provision. These, along with other schools' views, are covered in Chapter 6, 'Conclusions and Audit Check'.

Example 2: Reintegration for students from The Edith Borthwick School

During the latter stages of the project, students followed a programme of reintegration into their local mainstream schools at Year 9. One student, Youssef, had grown so much in confidence since the intensive thinking skills programmes and said:

I wasn't interested in doing a bit at special and a bit at mainstream – I knew I'd outgrown Edith Borthwick and I just wanted to get on with it. I knew I could cope with things now – I could think myself through the problems and that made it so much easier. I just told them, all of them, I wanted to go to mainstream full time and they said yes. I couldn't believe it – it was like I'd made it happen. When I got there it wasn't hard like I thought it would be. I could read better than lots of the others. I could also work out problems better, because I learnt it at Edith Borthwick. Some of my friends here couldn't think their way out of a paper bag and I can think my way out of the hardest problem you give me.

Teachers at Edith Borthwick had confirmed that Youssef was ready to move on. His integration links had been planned and started, but no-one was prepared for the sudden decision he made to go full time into a mainstream setting. One teacher said:

He became more and more assertive, almost aggressive at times. His reading age has increased by two years since the start of this thinking skills programme. This might not be attributable just to the thinking skills programme – he's been following intensive reading programmes as well. It's his appetite for learning, his confidence, his determination, when before he would give up.

Youssef still attends mainstream school and is studying for his GCSEs.

Conclusions

Many of the findings of the schools involved in this chapter are expanded in Chapter 5, 'Evaluation and Implications'. There follows a summary of individual school conclusions.

The Edith Borthwick School

Teachers have documented the changing nature of learners through the application of thinking skills programmes, describing them as 'more autonomous' and as recognising their own strengths and weaknesses and being able to determine their own learning priorities. They have seen thinking skills embedded into practice and now taught through a number of subjects across the curriculum. Specific targets related to thinking skills and problem-solving appear on most IEPs.

Staff have needed to extend their own range of skills in organising and managing teaching and learning. The quality of student and teacher interaction in the school is very much at the core of this more flexible approach; it is based on mutual trust and empathy rather than direct control. As negotiation, choice, and empowerment have become a part of the learning process, so trust and academic or personal guidance develop. The teacher's traditional role has extended to that of manager, organiser, resource, guide, counsellor, and tutor.

Longview Unit

Staff at Longview realised their target of changing the focus of the way they conceptualised and delivered learning programmes. They report the high involvement of pupils in this reconceptualisation. Programmes are now more relevant to individual needs, relating more specifically to the skills required for successful reintegration. Thinking skills programmes are now embedded within the structure of the learning programme, accompanied by more effective assessment.

Longview's outreach programme has been developed through the project and funding has been secured to support its development in the future.

Staff are reflecting on the philosophical base of their work. They have undergone significant change in the way they have structured and presented learning programmes and are keen to continue exploring the successful cognitive approaches they have been so successful with during the project.

Market Field School

The use of specific thinking skills material has provided a platform for further development in student self-confidence and autonomy as learners. Staff report that the process of structuring and presenting the materials was a strong learning process, leading to review of the way in which subjects are delivered at Key Stages 3 and 4.

Students have changed and developed through the application of thinking skills programmes and approaches. Staff note higher levels of independence, confidence and cooperation in students who have been involved in the project.

The school concludes its report by stating:

The outcome of the project has been to confirm that the development of student self-esteem and social skills (including social language) should be a priority. The way forward will require an evaluation of the pastoral curriculum, staff training (mentoring, circle time), the setting up of a student council and a review of the opportunities available to students in terms of equality.

Priory School

The work undertaken by Priory School during the project has resulted in thinking skills programmes being embedded in the personal and social education curriculum, which is now an entitlement for all students. The school is planning to review the way other subjects are delivered in the light of student response to thinking skills programmes.

Observations of students involved in the project show their increased ability to stop and consider problems before taking action, and particularly their ability to work together in pairs and small groups in a much more cooperative way.

Their report asserts that:

The nature of pupils who experience emotional and behavioural difficulties often means that there is a mismatch between capabilities and expectations with both students and staff. Any tool that makes working in a collaborative way more effective should be fully explored. The teaching of thinking skills offers one such tool. Because of the pupil-centred emphasis implicit in most thinking skills materials, the pupil is invited to participate in a way that often assures a positive outcome, for the group as well as for the individual. All participating pupils can make a valid contribution. Such outcomes ensure a building of self-esteem and confidence. Effective group work is facilitated by teaching thinking skills.

Finally . . .

The evidence we have gathered throughout this section indicates that the teaching of thinking skills has a clear impact on the development of pupil self-esteem and self-confidence, and produces more empowered learners. The materials have been thought-provoking. They have instigated mind-shifts in staff, have challenged pupils and students and have helped provide a platform for more positive attitudes and new approaches to learning, as well as increased personal skills evidenced by positive learning and life outcomes for many of the pupils described in this section.

It is not surprising that thinking skills is prominent on the national education agenda once more. David Blunkett, prior to his speech to the North of England Education Conference on 5th January 2000, asserted that:

All the evidence shows that systematic teaching of thinking skills raises standards. So, this autumn we will pilot a professional development programme designed to ensure secondary teachers know how to teach thinking skills through their specific subject areas.

It is also interesting to note that, in the revised version of the *National Curriculum* (DfEE/QCA 1999), many of the aspects of work in this chapter are explicitly described, either as key skills or as thinking skills, which are embedded in the programmes of study for the various subjects of the National Curriculum (see Appendix 1).

The future looks positive.

CHAPTER 4

The Practice – Promoting involvement in institutional development

This chapter describes the work of participating schools in promoting pupil involvement in school development through:

- seeking pupils' views as part of the development of curriculum or pastoral policy;
- the use of circle-time at classroom level to increase pupil participation in class decisions and school-based issues;
- the involvement of pupils in decision-making about school developments through the work of school councils.

Introduction

The richness of the projects described in this book lies both in the imaginative ways in which teachers have involved pupils in the life of their schools and the wide-ranging impact of doing so. This chapter goes beyond the involvement of pupils in issues to do with their own learning, examining ways in which they have been included in processes that lead to changes at the institutional level. In some cases this was the explicit purpose of the activity but other examples show how initiatives to involve pupils can have an unexpected impact on school development. We describe how pupils have been included in decision-making about changes in their schools and how, through more indirect ways, their perceptions and opinions have influenced developments in curriculum and pastoral care systems.

In seeking to draw together the variety of strategies for involving pupils that have an impact on institutional development we are proposing a model best described as a continuum of participation. At the low end of participation, pupils' perceptions and opinions are gathered as evidence on which to base decisions about school development. Moving along the continuum there are more interactive methods of consulting with pupils about the need for, or content of, change. Towards the end of high-level participation there are strategies that give pupils a voice in decision-making processes. Conceptualised in this way, increasing levels of involvement are also expected to lead to greater empowerment of pupils. Clearly, when teachers not only consult with pupils but also engage them in making decisions there has been a considerable shift in the balance of power between teacher and learner. This is unlikely to be a sudden or necessarily intentional change but, as the schools described below have found, moving along the continuum becomes a natural process once a culture of listening to pupils has become embedded in the life of a school.

When the pupil voice is taken seriously there can be substantial gains in terms of the knowledge base and effectiveness of a school. As highlighted in Chapter 1 there is evidence that successful schools place an emphasis on *pupil rights and responsibilities* (Sammons *et al.* 1995). In the literature on school improvement there is increasing awareness of the value of pupils' views in providing insights into the need for change. Equally there is recognition that it is possible to engage with pupil perspectives in more sophisticated ways that can have greater impact on school development. Thiessen (1997), for example, proposes three levels of working with students: learning about their views (researching about pupils), acting on their behalf (advocacy), and working with them (pupils as co-researchers).

There is evidence to suggest that pupils across the education system are being increasingly involved in school development at the first level, through many forms of consumer survey that provide feedback to school managers. Pupil perceptions have been found to offer a significant challenge to those of the adults in schools and have influenced decisions about the need for change. At the same time as the projects described in this book were underway the host local education authority (Essex County Council) established a large-scale primary school improvement programme in which pupil perception data proved to be one of the most powerful levers for change. Fielding *et al.* (1999) report that pupil perception data were systematically collected across all schools and found to be one of the main triggers for taking action, sometimes on issues that staff had not anticipated. Gathering data about the nature and quality of pupils' lived experience of the curriculum and the broader life of the school never failed to have an impact on the subsequent work of the schools involved.

The nature of participation fostered within a school partly depends on the position pupils are considered to hold within it. Handy and Aitken (1986) suggest pupils can be construed as 'products' (shaped and developed by the organisation), 'clients' (beneficiaries who are served by it) or 'workers' (members of the organisation who cooperate in joint endeavours). In the prevailing achievement-driven agenda of mainstream education pupils are often described in 'product' terms, with externally determined learning targets rather than pupil needs or interests driving school development. Historically, special schools have placed greater emphasis on treating children as individuals and in some senses 'clients'. It may therefore be a more natural development for special schools to progress towards pupils becoming partners in making decisions about institutional change. However, there is a substantial additional challenge provided by the significant special educational needs of pupils, who may have difficulties verbalising their views and wishes.

This chapter gives examples of three levels of pupil involvement in school development, which reflect the continuum described above. First, we present the work of schools that sought pupils' views as part of their development of curriculum or pastoral policy. More active participation through the use of circle-time at the classroom level is then described. Last, there are reports from two schools that actively seek to involve pupils in decision-making about school developments through schools councils.

Seeking pupils' perspectives to influence school development

Example 1: Seeking pupils' perspectives to develop a sexual health education policy and curriculum

Teachers at Cedar Hall chose to involve pupils in a number of different ways during this project. One of the impacts of this has been to highlight the value of consulting with pupils when staff are planning and implementing curriculum changes. The first area in which pupil views were taken into account was the development of a sexual health education policy and curriculum. In seeking to consult with pupils the school was influenced by government guidance on the personal, social and health education curriculum which recognises that the values of those involved in personal and social development of pupils differ. This can lead to a 'search for common ground; to an emphasis on consultation; and to respect for the views and rights of individuals' (*Curriculum Matters; Personal and Social Education 5–16*, DES 1989a).

Recognising their crucial function in ensuring that there is active debate and concern for individual values within this curriculum area, Cedar Hall wished to involve pupils from the outset in determining which key issues should be prioritised. Before producing a policy on sex education the school undertook a consultation process involving questionnaires and meetings with pupils, parents, governors and teachers. They report:

> *In fact, the whole process of formulating this policy evolved through a series of debates and discussions. In many respects, these interactions were as important as the final written document ... Consultation before formulating policy is nothing new to educational reform, but for our purposes what was new was the equal emphasis and consideration that was given to the views of pupils.*

The process began with an audit of pupils' views in Years 8 and 10. Pupils in Year 8 had very little prior experience of formal sexual health education, so in order to achieve consistent understanding of what was being asked explanation was given to the pupils in groups. The classes were informed that the school was rethinking the way sex education should be taught and that just as their parents had the opportunity to express their opinions, the school was interested in pupils' thoughts and ideas. It was made clear that the questions would not be personal to them and that they were not obliged to give their views if they did not feel comfortable in doing so, or did not wish to. Pupils were also given the opportunity to talk with a teacher of the same sex.

Views were gathered through structured interviews during which a questionnaire was completed. Pupils were asked their views about the importance of sexual health education and whether it should be taught in single-sex classes. They were also asked to comment on whether specific issues should be included in the curriculum. The questions asked and a summary of the pupil responses are shown as Figure 3.1.

All but one pupil (who did not wish to be interviewed) said that sex education was important and older pupils referred to the value for their life in the future. Two pupils mentioned specifically the importance of sex education taking place in school, because of the lack of opportunity to learn about it elsewhere. As a girl in Year 8 explained, 'It is important because some people can't learn about it at home'. A boy in Year 10 said, 'You are not going to get lessons when you have left school'.

On the issue of single-sex teaching there was a considerable split in opinion. All the girls but only 39% of boys wanted this. The comment made by one girl that

---

Sex education – Pupil questionnaire and findings

1. Do you think sex education is important?   Yes: 26(96%) No: 1(4%)

2. Why?   (See comments below)

3. Should it be taught in separate groups for boys and girls?

   Separate lessons: 100% of girls
   Mixed-sex lessons: 61% of boys

4. If you wanted advice about a sexual matter, who would you go to?

   (a) A friend: 6(21%)
   (b) Your parents: 10(36%)
   (c) A teacher: 1(4%)
   (d) Brother or sister: 2(7%)
   (e) Someone else: 6(21%)
   (f) Nobody: 3(11%)

5. Should the following things be discussed in class, and if so, when?

   Yes responses:
   Changes in our bodies: 25(96%)
   Boy/girlfriend going out: 19(73%)
   Ways of stopping pregnancy: 23(88%)
   How to say 'No' when someone is pressurising you: 21(81%)
   When sex is right and when it is wrong: 22(85%)
   Diseases you can catch from having sex: 25(96%)

Figure 3.1 Cedar Hall School sex education pupil questionnaire findings

boys tend to 'muck around and not take it seriously' was significant. As a direct consequence of the request from pupils, staff and governors, some opportunities for separate sexual health education were set up.

Question 5 raised an important issue about the appropriateness of consulting pupils on curriculum content. It could be argued that that students are not able to comment meaningfully on what should be included or when a subject should be taught if they have very little relevant prior knowledge. In fact in this subject area it was thought likely that pupils had some knowledge of the issues raised from earlier input in school and information 'picked up' from friends, home and the media. The vehemence of pupil responses to the questionnaire suggests they do in fact have much to say about the issue of sex education and their views are not automatically at odds with those of adults.

Of equal importance is the issue of enabling pupils to respond to questions that might present difficulties in terms of literacy demands or conceptual content. The questions were carefully constructed with this in mind and the quality of responses suggests they were successful in this. Significantly, the decision to present question-naires in individual interviews allowed adult support where accessibility was difficult. However, this approach also raises the question of potential adult bias influencing the views expressed by pupils.

In summarising the impact of consulting pupils on this area of curriculum development the school reported:

> We believe this to be just a start. This relatively small step of including pupils' ideas and views in planning the curriculum has required, in one sense, a whole shift in approach. Instead of the pupils being viewed as 'done to' they are steadily being given more responsibility and their views listened to. Pupils are increasingly shaping their own lives. If we are to properly prepare our pupils for citizenship in a democracy, where listening and taking account of each other's views is so important, then surely this is a way forward. Adults listening to and taking pupils seriously can only be a good role model for the younger generation to emulate.

Example 2: Seeking pupils' perspectives to develop a thinking skills policy

The rationale for developing thinking skills as the core of pupils' educational experience at Longview is described in the previous chapter. In the process of build-ing their thinking skills programme a number of published materials were trialled and evaluated through staff and pupil feedback. Given the individualised nature of the curriculum being developed, pupils' views were essential in determining which elements of the published schemes were most valuable.

Pupil feedback was sought in two ways. Firstly, programmes were monitored through weekly entries in pupils' Record of Achievement folders, which recorded how a young person used the session and whether they had any particular difficulties. Secondly, pupil evaluations of the programme as a whole took place through group discussions and individual interviews. Staff at Longview found that seeking pupils' views through questionnaires achieved limited, often only one-word, responses. The most effective method was the individual interview, taped if necessary, and then written up to be approved and signed by the young person concerned. This seemed to be a less threatening process for the pupils and resulted in more detailed and thoughtful responses. Interviews used a structured format, which meant effectively delivering a spoken questionnaire. This method, also used in the example above, provided a degree of consistency but also flexibility in allowing the interviewer to vary the order of questions if appropriate and to offer explanation of anything the young person does not understand. With questionnaires it is common for respondents to give up quickly rather than ponder the meaning of a question. Below are the questions staff at Longview used in their evaluation of the two thinking skills programmes:

Did you enjoy the programme?
What did you find most enjoyable?
What have you learned about yourself?
What have you learned about your thinking skills?
What skills did you find easiest?
What skills did you find hardest?
What would you like to work further on?
Do you think you have applied these skills to any other areas of your life?
Do you have any other comments you would like to make about this programme?

Another innovative method used to gather pupils' views was to combine group discussions with individual completion of questionnaires. This had the benefit of students stimulating each other's thoughts through discussion and recollection. Below are examples of comments made by pupils.

The opportunity to think around why things may have happened and what could have been done differently.

Good communication was useful. I have definitely developed skills and recognised the importance of correct and careful communication.

Thinking around use of eye contact and body language has been helpful particularly in recognising the signs in others. It's often easy to misinterpret signs and I think I've learnt to think again and be aware of the possibility of misreading things in others.

What I am taking away with me from these programmes is the confidence to speak out and say clearly what I really think. This has particularly helped to get me back to school.

Example 3: Seeking pupils' perspectives to develop pupil support systems

At Edith Borthwick a student survey has been used to track a focused year group of pupils annually over a three-year period. Pupils have completed a questionnaire as part of their personal, social and health education programme. They have been supported throughout and confidentiality has been assured. Pupils have also been made aware that the purpose of the information obtained is to track progress and that a parallel staff consultation process has taken place.

The questionnaire consists of three sets of statements to which pupils indicate agreement or disagreement. The statements, grouped under the headings *About Me*, *About School* and *About My Social Life* are all directed at the pupils' personal experience, referring to *I* or *Me*. The statements, results in 1994 and a comparison with 1997 are reproduced in Appendix 10.

Initial responses to the questionnaire were predominantly negative and unexpected by school staff. The effect of a discrepancy between staff and pupils' perceptions served to galvanise school developments in order to address the arising issues. For example, data in the *About Me* section suggested there were significant issues with regard to indications of low self-esteem, lack of trust and confidence, and inability to deal with feelings of anger or frustration. These resulted in a substantial range of developments including the following teaching and support/guidance strategies:

- *Increased team-building activities within physical education and personal, social and health education.*
- *General increase in group work.*
- *Active pursuance of student self-awareness through focused feedback in support and guidance tutorials.*
- *Use of student mentoring (buddying).*
- *Increased personal, social and health education development in the primary years.*
- *Setting of short-term targets and teaching of specific personal skills.*
- *Structured post-16 transition programme that enables students to make informed decisions.*
- *Clear and consistent expectations and sanctions across the school with regard to student behaviour.*
- *Behaviour management plans for individual pupils.*
- *Student negotiation and input into annual reviews.*

Responses from pupils to the *About School* section indicated some significant areas of concern that the school needed to address. Summarising the findings and implications of the questionnaire, the school reported:

The management and nature of student behaviour is fundamental to the majority of student responses. These essentially reflect disaffection within the school environment. The largest collective response (64%) indicates that some students are afraid of other people in the school. With only one student (4%) indicating discrimination by teachers it is most likely that students are having problems with each other. This conclusion is supported by the students that admit to bullying one another (36%), and by those who indicate that they have no friends at school (44%). A stronger

PSHE programme implemented within the primary years would help to lay the foundation for a more cohesive and caring student population in later key stages.

More than half the sample (60%) recognise that they make life difficult for teachers. The majority (52%) indicate that they do not like to be told what to do by teaching staff. 40% of students feel that they do not always pay attention in class, a corresponding sample (40%) admit to missing lessons on a whole lesson or part lesson basis. This high figure may be reflected within the 52% who feel they are frequently late in getting to school. This may have been interpreted as being late for class rather than school. There are clear indicators here for the closer monitoring of school transport, the development of more effective teaching and learning strategies, and also for targeted short term student support and guidance in which expectations are clearly given, and consistently followed up.

The majority of students (64%) indicate that the work is not always pitched at the correct level with 36% finding it too easy, and 28% too hard. This means that the work offered within Years 7/11 is correctly structured for only 36% of students according to student perception. There are clear indicators here for more effective differentiation. Curriculum support, consolidation, and extension work needs to be apparent within learning programmes.

Some students indicate that they would rather not be at school (32%), with a further 28% of the same sample showing a preference for a different school. The same 32% of students admit to causing damage to the fabric of the school. This reflects the number of students who feel that they are singled out and treated differently (32%).

According to student perceptions a minority display extreme disaffected behaviour. Teachers within these year groups feel that this is an honest and accurate portrayal. The way forward for these students can be found within individual counselling, guidance, and target setting. It does require commitment from both school, home, and student. It is costly in terms of staff time, and is potentially emotionally unsettling for the student to have self-imposed barriers removed.

In the section *About My Social Life* there were strong indications of loneliness, lack of friends and dissatisfaction with the home environment. This led to a range of changes including the introduction of a school-based youth club, an increased range of residential activities and closer parental contact.

The action research approach not only provided a catalyst for institutional change but also provided evidence of the impact of these developments. As the differences between responses in 1997 and 1994 show, the data support the adult perspective that there has been a considerable positive shift in pupil self-esteem and attitude to school. For example fewer pupils were afraid of others and more had friends in school. Fewer were worried about the future or said they didn't have enough friends. The school reported:

It is most likely that all of the strategies and practices that have been initiated during the last four years have in some ways reshaped and influenced school culture for our students. The original target group indicates an upward shift. However, student attitudes and perceptions indicate ongoing problems with self-esteem within our current Year 7 group, particularly for those students who have transferred from mainstream at the time of primary/secondary transition . . . Perhaps the most significant outcome of the action research has been the clarification of the disaffection and self-esteem problem from the pupil perspective.

Example 4: Seeking pupils' perspectives to develop individual education planning

The Heath School prioritised the involvement of pupils in negotiating targets and participating in reviews, described in Chapter 2, 'Pupils as partners'. They sought feedback from pupils as the primary source of evidence for evaluating the effectiveness of the project. Staff set out to interview two pupils from each of the year groups involved in the project, Years 7 to 10. The pupils were interviewed individually and asked to describe their feelings and opinions in relation to the process they had been through.

Each interview followed a similar format and addressed three main areas of enquiry. Firstly, staff asked a series of questions relating to the period of time prior to the implementation of the participatory individual education planning process in the school. It was hoped that the following questions would yield some insights into pupils' recollections of practice before the start of the project in order to establish some sort of baseline:

- Were you aware of any targets that you had before you had an individual education plan?
- Did these targets relate to your statement; your Annual Review; or other issues?
- How were you made aware of these targets?
- Did anyone ever talk to you about these targets? If so, when?
- Did these targets mean anything to you?

In response to these questions, only two of the pupils could recall having targets before being involved in an individual education plan as part of the project. Of these two pupils, neither felt that the targets were discussed in any detail over the course of a school year or that the targets had any real meaning to them.

Next, staff asked questions relating to the present. The following questions were asked in order to try to find out about pupils' responses to the process of participating in the development of an individual education plan:

- What do you think is the purpose of your individual education plan?
- Are you aware of all your targets now?
- Do you feel that having an individual education plan helps you?
- How much are you involved in setting your targets?

- Is this involvement important to you?
- How much support do you get from staff to help you reach your targets?
- How much information do you get as to how well you are doing?
- Do you get this information:
  - at the end of class?
  - at the end of each session?
  - through the black folder?
  - from the round-robin?
- Is this information enough?
- Is the information useful?
- Do you get information when the target is not one for in class?

In reporting the results of this phase of the pupil interviews, staff at The Heath School wrote:

> When the pupils were asked about the current situation all were able to recount their IEP targets. This was very enlightening and a very positive aspect. Three quarters of the pupils felt that the IEP had helped them in some way which was also very positive.

The fact that every one of the pupils was able to give valid explanations as to the purpose of an individual education plan was also seen as very positive. Pupils suggested that the purposes of individual education plans include:

> to help me improve on areas of weakness and socialising;
> to help us achieve . . . get back on track and to learn more;
> for me and my teacher to become more aware of my needs and what to work on;
> to help me on things I have problems with.

The responses to the questions focusing on pupil involvement in the targets were also revealing. Five pupils said that they felt totally involved in the process of setting targets in their individual education plans; two pupils reported a sense of being partially involved; one pupil had no sense of involvement at all. When they were subsequently asked if the sense of involvement was important to them, seven of the eight pupils said 'yes', giving a strong indication of the importance that pupils attach to involvement once they have experienced it.

During the middle phase of the interviews, all the pupils said that they were satisfied with the levels of staff support they received in helping them to reach their targets. One pupil indicated that this support could sometimes turn into 'nagging'.

In response to the questions regarding feedback, the pupils were critical. The interviewees at The Heath School felt that they did not receive enough information at the end of an 'out of class' session. As a result, half of those asked did not feel the feedback information was adequate, even though three quarters of the pupils felt the information was useful.

When asked about the benefits of having an individual education plan, the responses were again very positive. Seven pupils were of the opinion that they had benefited from their individual education plan. When asked to summarise the benefits of being involved in their own individual education plans, all seven pupils gave coherent justifications for their opinions, including:

My targets have helped me get higher points.
They help to remind me of what I'm working towards.
They have made me stop and think before I say things.
I'm getting more sensible and I feel proud and pleased when I get them right but sometimes if I get ". . . . ." I think oh sod it and I no longer care.
It makes me feel better when I get it right.

The third phase of the interview focused on the future. In order to canvass pupils' views on ways of refining and improving practice in relation to individual education planning, staff asked pupils the following questions:

- Do you think you have benefited from having an IEP?
- If so, in what ways?
- Do you feel that the pupils who have not had an IEP up until now have missed out in any way?
- If so, in what ways?
- Have you any suggestions as to how we could improve the ways we work with pupils at The Heath School in order to make individual education planning better?

The positive feelings expressed by pupils about the benefits of individual education plans in the middle phase of the interviews were carried over into the responses to the final set of questions. When the interviewees were asked to compare their experiences with those of pupils who were not yet working on an individual education plan, three quarters of the group felt that these pupils were missing out. The pupils were again able to give well argued explanations in support of their feelings, including:

You get higher points for doing your IEP.
They have not been able to improve their weaknesses.
They need help in certain areas too.
If they have a special target it could help them to achieve it.

Half the pupils interviewed also suggested improvements to the individual education planning process. Interestingly, these pupils all recommended increasing the frequency of feedback for 'out of class' sessions.

Taken together, staff at The Heath School regarded the outcomes of the pupil interviews as extremely enlightening in terms of the impact of the 'Involving Pupils' project. They also reported their sense of pleasure at the extent to which the pupils involved in the project:

- appeared to feel comfortable enough to share their honest views;
- made predominantly positive statements about the process of being involved;

- expressed their interest and motivation through suggested improvements for future practice in relation to individual education plans which focused on increased levels of pupil involvement.

Building pupil involvement and influence through Circle-Time

At Cedar Hall School Circle-Time had a significant influence in its development towards a pupil-centred culture. Introduced into the school in September 1996, this initiative aimed to teach pupils to communicate with each other effectively, to teach them the art of listening and of expressing their feelings, opinions and even their fears publicly.

During Circle-Time pupils and adults sit together in a circle and each takes a turn to speak on a particular issue, abiding by these agreed rules:

- Only talk one at a time.
- Be kind and don't say anything that will hurt anybody.
- Listen carefully.
- Talk clearly so everyone can hear you.

With younger children sometimes a 'special' object may be passed around the circle and only the person with the object may speak. If anyone does not want to contribute to the discussion they say 'pass' and the object moves on. By adopting this simple technique it has been used effectively with everyone from the youngest class of reception children to the Year 11 leavers' classes. It can be used simply to play games or tell stories round the class, inform each other of events that happened at the weekend or share personal goals. At other times it is used to discuss disciplinary procedures such as rules, rewards and punishments. For example, when a new lunch time policy was being put in place the pupils in each class were asked to decide what sanctions and rewards should be associated with the midday assistant's 'Disappointment and Congratulations Slips'.

Staff at Cedar Hall have found that using Circle-Time to involve pupils in developing behaviour management strategies has proved successful in reducing the number of discipline issues in the playground. Pupils now take ownership of the rules. Less intervention is needed from adults because peer pressure, guided and regulated by staff, appears to be far more effective at changing behaviour. Beyond this the impact has been more far-reaching in supporting a cultural shift in the school. In their report Cedar Hall quote the deputy head teacher's view that 'Circle-Time has been so successful because it has enabled the whole school community to communicate better'. The following exert from the school report provides a powerful demonstration of this change, which began as much from pupils asserting their own wish to have a say as from adults offering them the opportunity to do so.

A topic of conversation guaranteed to arise regularly in a staff room, or for that matter playground of any school, is the topic of uniform. It did not surprise the staff, therefore, when in the Autumn Term 1995 the girls from Year 11 began discussing amongst themselves how unfair it was that they were not allowed to wear trousers, in contrast to their counterparts in most mainstream schools. What was surprising, however, was the sensible and organised way that they went about bringing their complaint to the senior management team. After discussion with the school counsellor they wrote a petition, and together with clipboards lent by a sympathetic female member of staff, went about gaining popular support by asking for signatures from their peers. Such was their clamour for change that it could not be ignored and to the dismay of some parents, who had recently invested in new skirts, the uniform was changed. The girls had equal rights and they knew it, they had fought and won! Overnight those girls grew in stature. Their self-confidence boosted, they proudly strutted around the playground showing off their newly acquired uniform.

The boys, not to be outdone, quickly organised themselves to petition for white trainers to be allowed. After all, they argued, these would increase their safety walking home in the dark and surely this must be a priority to the school! They were not so lucky. Black shoes were to remain the standard uniform. Bright reflective jackets had always been allowed, as the head teacher clearly pointed out in the following assembly. He went on to say how proud he felt, however, that the pupils had taken the initiative and taken action to try and bring about change.

In a matter of days a new phase in the school's history had begun to be ushered in. Pupils began to realise that pupils could have a 'say' in the running of their school.

Staff too began to consult and involve pupils in areas where previously they themselves would have made the decisions. Some notable examples being involving pupils in designing the new adventure playground in June 1997, by putting several plans to the pupils for a vote. More recently in the past term, having been provided with £1,000 by the Government to buy books, it was decided to allow every pupil the opportunity to choose a book at a local book shop to supplement the library. Consequently pupils seem to have much more of a sense of ownership of these particular books. Alex, a Year 8 pupil, said of the initiative: 'It was a good idea because instead of the teachers having to rack their brains to decide what books pupils like to read, they asked us because after all we know.'

Participation in decision-making – the school council

School councils have had a chequered history over the last twenty years. A survey in 1993 (ACE 1995) found that only a seventh of primary schools and 50 per cent of secondary schools ran school councils. When compared to a similar survey in 1989 in which 97 per cent of secondary schools responding had school councils, this suggests a reduction of interest in pupil participation. In the ACE survey some schools reported that the demands of the National Curriculum and a shift away from 'pupil-focused' practice had reduced the time for pupil involvement in decision-making. However others felt the move towards local management freed them up to choose to set up a council if they wished. There are recent signs of a renewal of interest in school councils across the educational spectrum.

The following examples demonstrate the organic nature of such structures which perhaps explains their fragility in a rapidly changing educational context.

The first account is a brief description of a recently developed school council while the second describes a council that has been in operation for some years but which has changed considerably during the life of this project. This is described in some detail in order to explain how the council developed from a relatively ineffective meeting to a genuine vehicle for pupil participation in decision making.

Example 1: Cedar Hall School

At Cedar Hall School the wish for better communication throughout the school lead to the development of a democratically elected school council. This was established in December 1997 with a boy and a girl representing each year group. Their job was to bring to the attention of the council issues discussed at a class level that relate to the whole school. Initially the council met once a month during lunch times, but recently this has been increased to once a fortnight, during Assemblies, in order to give more time for discussion and to avoid a clash with extracurricular activities. A member of staff from both the upper and lower school sit in on the meetings, which were initially chaired by a teacher. However, a secretary and chairman have now been elected from among the pupils and the staff aim to take more of a back seat in the proceedings. Some of the actions arising from issues raised by pupils are:

- developing a tuck shop to be run by pupils;
- providing hymn-books for Class 1 like the rest of the school;
- fairer supervision of the adventure playground;
- more non-school uniform days.

The council is in its infancy, but the enthusiasm and persistence of the pupils involved has encouraged its further development. The school reports that pupils are beginning to think for themselves and there is increasing willingness to allow them to take responsibility for making improvements to the quality of daily life within the school.

Example 2: Hayward School

Hayward School has a longer established school council; however feedback from their pupils two years earlier indicated that it was not working effectively. Staff concurred with this view and because the school was at that time reassessing its aims and direction the council was disbanded, giving time to consider how it could be improved. At the centre of the dissatisfaction with the council was the election of its representatives. At that time there were in the school some very dominant boys who almost became self-elected. The council was good for their self-esteem, but they did not take seriously the responsibility of listening to and representing the views of others.

Staff and pupils took some time to discuss a better election model. It was decided that beforehand pupils would receive a curriculum module on citizenship within their tutor groups. There would then be a ballot to choose a representative whom peers felt would be best at listening to them, representing their views at the council, and involving them in the outcome. In order to support and develop these skills, the following organisational strategies were put into place:

- time given to discussing the school council in PSE lessons;
- agendas and minutes sent to the representatives and class tutors;
- the outcomes of the school council to be mentioned in Assemblies.

It was agreed to be straightforward with pupils about access to funds, and to encourage them to discuss all issues, but then divide them into 'dreams' (make the swimming pool deeper) and 'realities' (more footballs for playtime). The school council also began to debate issues other than those involving resources. Previous agendas tended to be 'want lists': however, they now began to discuss issues of atmosphere, ethos and attitude in the school. For example, recent agendas have included debates about how the school could best welcome and include a new autism resource base. The school reported:

A visitor to one of these meetings told us how impressed he was by our students' use and understanding of the term 'autism' and their readiness to talk sympathetically about generalisations they can already draw about the behaviour of those of their peers whom they know to be autistic. As a response to these debates, we have begun signing during assemblies and each class has a programme of autism awareness activities.

The evolution of the school council has continued and it now has its own budget. This was initially spent on replacing lost and damaged playground equipment such as footballs, basketballs and skipping-ropes but representatives are beginning to talk about organising their own fund-raising events in order to increase their spending power.

Many of the requests of the school council have achieved positive outcomes. For example, reports from representatives of any vandalism to pupils' toilets are responded to instantly. The council have instigated a rota of students prepared to have a watching eye over behaviour in the toilets at breaktimes, resulting in improved conditions. A recurrent request for playground furniture resulted in the school providing hard-standing and sturdy picnic benches, and the Friends of the school funded a wooden and chain play trail of bridges, balances and swings. Details of the planning of these projects as they went along, including costs, were posted on the student notice board. Overall there have been a wide range of issues addressed as a result of their being raised by the school council, including:-

- *improved girls' changing rooms;*
- *playground furniture;*

- *lunch time clubs;*
- *improved wildlife gardens;*
- *pupils questioned on school uniform (requests for a blazer were not supported by the majority);*
- *5 MPH signs for taxis driving on site;*
- *more pupils' art work displayed around the school (the school now has a 'gallery' – a long, wide corridor with spotlights playing onto students' framed work);*
- *autism awareness programme;*
- *staff not to talk to each other while on playground duty (pupils quite rightly noted that while we talked to each other we were not noticing what was going on around the playground);*
- *new fence;*
- *use of new library (representatives wanted to be assured that there would be access for all pupils of the school).*

This list of achievements represents considerable success in itself. However, the school also sought to evaluate its impact from the pupils' perspective. Before the changes described took place, most pupils knew very little if anything about the school council. There were others who knew and understood the process but did not feel involved in it. The overwhelming view was that although most pupils knew of the existence of the school council, they were not aware of what was being discussed or of any tangible outcomes.

After four terms of the new model PSE time was used to debate the effects of the school council, and pupils completed a questionnaire. All pupils from Year 4 and above who were in school that day took part, 78 in all. The responses were as follows:

1. *Most pupils knew who their school council representative was (93%).*

2. *A variety of reasons for choosing their representative were given:*

   - *he got the most votes;*
   - *he is good with answers and he argues about what we want;*
   - *she is reliable;*
   - *she is responsible.*

3. *What sort of things they asked their rep to bring to the school council:*

   - *things that make the school look better;*
   - *anything that we want;*
   - *things like the library and the playground;*
   - *what to do when footballs get kicked over the wall and we don't have any more to play with;*
   - *water fountain outside;*
   - *an alarm in the new library and information and communication technology room;*

- *better equipment;*
- *posters;*
- *benches outside;*
- *shower curtains;*
- *how to stop any bullying;*
- *towels in the girls' changing rooms;*
- *clubs.*

4. *Most felt that the school council helped to get things done (95%).*

5. *Most felt that the school council is a good idea (92%), for these reasons:*

- *you get some good ideas from it;*
- *it helps get things;*
- *it is something to be proud of;*
- *we can have a say in what we buy;*
- *children have their say instead of the adults;*
- *many of the ideas are used for school improvements;*
- *because we want to share our ideas;*
- *because they get us stuff like basketballs;*
- *it makes the school look better when people visit here.*

6. *Suggestions for improvement were:*

- *more reps (for example, there is currently one rep per class from Year 4 upwards);*
- *change reps twice a year;*
- *teachers to read the report back to the class;*
- *more teachers at the meetings;*
- *have more money to spend/raise money to help;*
- *meet more than once a term;*
- *have a boy and a girl rep from each class;*
- *other pupils to see what happens at a school council meeting.*

There were some negative responses. Some pupils felt that their views were not being listened to, and that the school was not responding to the requests of their council. Whilst these views were in the minority, the school consider there is still work to be done in making more explicit the issues raised by the council that have been taken forward by the school, for example through a school council newsletter. Nevertheless, staff at The Hayward consider the school council to have been a positive force in the school. They reported:

Over the past two years it has evolved and grown in response to pupil feedback, and will continue to do so. It is firmly pinned to the personal and social education curriculum and through class tutors involves all members of the classroom community. It encourages pupils to work as a group, to listen to the views of others, to trust someone to represent their view.

We feel that the ethos of the school has improved and that pupils and staff alike have a raised self-esteem. This has not been brought about solely by the development of the school council, but by a myriad of strategies and structures that staff felt were needed in order to improve the educational opportunities offered by the school. We are building a community where pupils enjoy sharing achievements and problem-solving together. Having time and support on the project to develop ideas regarding the school council has given us an important reminder to continually ask ourselves if we are involving pupils enough in the various routes we take.

All teachers are short of time, and we at The Hayward are no exception. With more time we could document so much more of the 'hidden curriculum' that is vital to our ethos of adults and pupils learning and supporting each other as a team. Using some slightly 'harder' data collection methods (pupil interviews, pupil questionnaires) has without question both given us greater insight into pupils' perceptions of the workings of the school and given pupils a greater feeling of being really involved in the shaping of their environment. We have every intention, therefore, of replicating these methods with other aspects of our practice.

Conclusions

At the beginning of this section we proposed a model of pupil participation that placed the range of strategies available for involving pupils in institutional development along a continuum. The intention was not to make value judgements about where a school lies on this dimension but to provide a means of describing the 'journey' some schools have taken. In one school (Cedar Hall) in particular there were examples of teachers engaging with pupils at all three levels. While this does not represent a simple progression from low to high level participation it is clear that as the staff recognised the value of consulting with pupils about curriculum issues they became more receptive to the notion of other forms of involvement. It is particularly interesting to note the role the pupils themselves played in influencing this development. By demonstrating that they had a voice the students' actions resulted in significant change in their own and teachers' expectations of the contribution they could make. In this school the success of one strategy lead to further experimentation, opening up additional areas of school life in which pupils were able to have a say.

At some schools increased involvement of pupils represented a substantial cultural change. For example, the final comments by staff at The Hayward School indicate that the development of an active school council coincided with the school's development of an ethos of collaboration among staff and pupils. The council had been in existence for some years but had become ineffective. The activity of pupils meeting with adults was not in itself sufficient to enable genuine participation. The pupils were not aware of the purpose of the council and had become disillusioned about what effect it might have. Their example demonstrates that for a school council to be effective it must show that pupils' contributions are taken seriously. In the context of increased collaboration the school council blossomed and played a substantial role in enabling and sustaining the change in culture.

A further implication of the work described above was the impact of involving pupils at a level beyond their individual interests. The intention of engaging pupils in discussion about curriculum content or the social organisation of a school was to make more effective institutional change. However these processes also had significant impact on the pupils themselves. The opportunity to take part in discussions, give opinions and listen to others' views, provided by the work in these schools, lies at the heart of the recently developed citizenship curriculum (DfEE/QCA 1999). The impact on pupil's self-esteem, confidence and experience of articulating their views was such that these can no longer be seen as peripheral activities. They offer a real-life context for pupils to learn and practise skills for citizenship.

CHAPTER 5

Evaluation and Implications

Introduction

In this chapter we gather evaluative comments from each of the participating schools and include implications arising from the various outcomes. Evaluations include direct quotes from project schools' final reports, further materials supplied by several schools during the writing of this book and comments from the authors.

We have grouped the evaluations under the following headings in order to help guide the reader:

- Implications for pupils and students
- Implications for reintegration and inclusion
- Impact on staff
- Impact on the curriculum
- Issues in school development
- Reflections on data-gathering methods.

Implications for pupils and students

Raised assertiveness and confidence

One of the outcomes of the project, observed in different ways across the schools, was a demonstration of enhanced assertiveness and confidence among students to make suggestions for changes to organisational structures, particularly in those providing for pupil support. Perhaps pupils' perceptions of the receptiveness of staff to such ideas had also changed through positive experience of being given a voice.

A recent example from one school suggests that students have internalised the principles of Circle-Time. One of the Year 10 pupils asked whether she and her friends could run a pupil-to-pupil listening service, to try and relieve the school counsellor whose time, in her opinion, was being overstretched trying to deal with higher priority problems.

In a school where thinking skills had been highly developed, two students agreed to deliver part of a training day on thinking skills for the local education authority. The day was attended by teachers and learning support assistants and the two students taught them how to be successful with some *Instrumental Enrichment* exercises. Evaluation at the end of the course gave the highest rating to this particular workshop. The students said that they felt valued and respected and also considered themselves to be teachers. Another student from the same group was invited to talk to a group of professionals at a careers and business partnership conference about a volunteer scheme running in his school. He gave an authoritative and assertive presentation, using a powerpoint presentation accompanied by facts and anecdotes. When asked why he seemed so confident he said, 'It was easy. I just stop, think about the problem, work it out in my mind and draw it in pictures. I then remember the pictures. The powerpoint was fun.'

The teaching of thinking skills resulted in changes in self-confidence and assertiveness for pupils in several schools. One example shows a teacher reflecting on the class after the use of a particular programme over a period of time:

> *It was noted that the students showed improved involvement in group activities over the period of time covered and this was particularly true of the students who had been very self-conscious and shy at the outset. Students have grown in confidence in the whole-class discussion/debate situation. Certain students have begun to develop their use of reasoned argument to influence other people's opinions.*

In another school, the project coordinator makes links between the nature of thinking skills programmes and the growth of self-confidence in pupils:

> *In the wider context, the teaching of thinking skills can be seen to influence the way a child will react to any new task, once the concept of 'wait a minute – let me think' is well enough established.*

> *Many pupils already make good progress using this strategy in structured and unstructured situations. The effect can be seen in most personal and social education lessons where the association is currently strongest.*

> *The nature of pupils who experience emotional and behavioural difficulties often means that there is a mismatch between capabilities and expectations with both students and staff. Any tool that makes working in a collaborative way more effective should be fully explored. The teaching of thinking skills offers one such tool. Because of the pupil-centred emphasis implicit in most thinking skills materials, the pupil is invited to participate in a way that often assures a positive outcome, for the group as well as for the individual. All participating pupils can make a valid contribution. Such outcomes ensure a building of self-esteem and confidence. Effective group work is facilitated by teaching thinking skills.*

Another project coordinator, heavily involved with the development of thinking skills, notes that, 'In essence many students have started to develop as autonomous learners, recognising their own strengths and weaknesses, and determining their own learning priorities'. Two students from this school proved their new-found assertiveness by negotiating their passage into a mainstream school.

There are, however, potential conflicts which may arise where pupils are empowered in the school and where school staff find themselves acting as advocates on behalf of pupils, especially with parents who may not share the views or aspirations of the school. Conflicts could arise in legal situations where parents have more rights than children. Similarly, conflicts with colleagues may arise where pupils make value judgements about teaching content or the effectiveness of teachers.

Schools where there is a high belief in pupil involvement will already be considering the implications of such tensions, for example through parent partnership schemes, through the policies, structures and protocols communicated to staff, parents and pupils, through clear and transparent communication systems and, most importantly, through responsive and sensitive approaches to the curriculum.

Increased opportunities to express opinions

One of the most effective methods of enabling and encouraging pupils to express their opinions in matters relating to their education and welfare is the school council. In the words of some of the pupils voted onto one school council, the purpose of this forum is:

> to voice the opinions of children, the voice of everyone to get things done. It proves that you can be grown up. It's a very good thing. It is giving other people the chance to have their say.

In three schools a major outcome of the project has been the quality of suggestions pupils have made about improving the school council system. These schools also articulate an increased sense of purpose within the school council, evidenced by clearer and more focused decision-making by students, less need for adult guidance and support, more ideas about extending the remit of the school council and more informed views about how the school works accompanied by more realistic expectations of how to bring about change.

In two schools pupils expressed clear views about the way adults were working with them, the kind of materials that were used and the kind of teaching styles that were favoured by teaching staff. In one school, this led to the development of thinking skills programmes and more individualised teaching programmes as a result of pupil preference. A further positive outcome was an increase in pupils' ability to reintegrate into mainstream provision as a direct result of more appropriate learning programmes and personal support.

In the other school, the views of pupils about their own self-esteem led to a major review of the way the secondary curriculum was delivered, including changes to subject delivery (for example, the introduction of thinking skills across several subjects), more flexible teaching and learning styles (for example increased team-teaching, paired and small group work, increased use of information and communication technology), developments in pastoral and guidance systems (for example individual action planning, the employment of a school counsellor) and the introduction of a school council.

Increased enthusiasm and motivation to become participants

In one school the hallmark of the school council is the enthusiasm which the pupils bring to the meetings. Staff report that representatives frequently check when the council will meet next, to the extent that, to a busy teacher, their eagerness can even become a nuisance.

The positive attitude of the pupils themselves has therefore become the flywheel that keeps the momentum of the council going. This is fuelled by the experience of positive results to requests for change, linked with the endorsement of the council from staff, for example by referring to the council in assemblies. This flywheel image is crucial to the success of the council. It will not embed into practice as a staff-driven initiative. It must win pupils' confidence and support.

Quite often pupils not only have original solutions to problems, for example, banning the tuck shop if litter were ever to become a problem, but they also often see difficulties that adults may not. At a school council meeting, a Year 9 pupil spontaneously suggested that more basketballs should be provided for the playground at breaktime. She had noticed that competition for balls was becoming a problem – staff had not.

Where involvement in planning has been a focus, evidence of increased enthusiasm among pupils for taking part in review has also been shown. For example, in one school where a lot of work was done on involving pupils in individual education planning, there is now one hundred per cent attendance, by choice, of pupils at their Annual Reviews.

Increased knowledge and ownership of target setting

In schools where there had been a focus on increasing opportunities for pupils to be involved in setting targets, staff reported a number of positive advantages. In one school, the simple fact of setting up individual education plans for all pupils, and ensuring that all pupils are involved in setting targets and reviewing progress, was seen as a major step forward. This school also noted that the pupils themselves, as a result of work done during the 'Involving Pupils' project, have learned to value their individual education plans as having a significant role to play in meeting their priority needs. Staff and pupils mean to work together to build on this success and to seek to improve the shared process of monitoring progress towards targets.

Other schools noted that pupils were initially resistant to the idea of negotiating their own targets with staff – possibly because they anticipated conflict arising between their self-set targets and those identified by members of staff. Involvement in the project enabled staff and pupils to work through these difficulties and to arrive at a point where targets are set collaboratively without compromising a genuine sense of pupil ownership.

In several schools, pupils' doubts about the value of targets were overcome when they began to see very positive results. Pupils, as well as staff, began to realise that working towards explicit targets contributed to a perceptible reduction in the need for both incident reporting and individual action plans focused on difficulties over behaviour. As we have shown in Chapter 4 'Promoting involvement in institutional development', pupils also felt positively motivated by the possibility of measuring their own progress towards targets, either by collecting staff comments for themselves or by building up reward points.

Staff in at least one school also noted the importance of the process of discussing targets with pupils. Providing good quality tutorial time, with a member of staff in a mentoring role, gave pupils a new outlet for the expression of confused and challenging emotions. Simply talking things through with a trusted member of staff on a regular basis, with targets as a focus for discussion, reduced incidents of challenge and aggression in other contexts. Staff also used tutorials focused on targets as a forum for giving pupils conscious techniques for coping with their difficulties as they arose. This combination of mentoring, shared target setting and direct guidance in self-management strategies proved to be time-intensive but highly effective.

Implications for reintegration and inclusion

One school, which regularly reintegrates pupils into the mainstream, sends an evaluation questionnaire to mainstream schools 21 working days after pupils have been discharged back into the mainstream or after the final outreach visit. This questionnaire is designed to follow up a number of the questions which are asked about pupils on their admission and could therefore be said to measure the impact which has been made upon pupils' difficulties. Among the comments gathered in this way are the following:

She has become very outgoing and supportive of other students (said of a student with anorexia in Year 10 who is now fully reintegrated into a mainstream school).

She has raised levels of self-esteem and confidence. More personal insights. (said of a student in Year 9 who had been suicidal and is now fully reintegrated into a mainstream school).

Increase in self-esteem. Not quite as late in the morning! (said of a girl in Year 8 with obsessive compulsive disorder who is now fully reintegrated into a mainstream school).

He has gained in confidence – he looks fitter! (said of a boy in Year 10 who had been suicidal and who has now achieved partial reintegration).

She is enjoying school and says she is pleasantly surprised by the number of new friends she has made (said of a student with anorexia in Year 10 who has now achieved partial reintegration).

She seems relaxed, settled (said of a student with anorexia in Year 11 who has now achieved partial reintegration).

She is definitely happier at school and her general demeanour appears more positive and upbeat (said of a student in Year 11 who had been suicidal but who has now achieved full reintegration).

She is much more able to cope with life in general (said of a student in Year 9 who had been very withdrawn and refused to attend school – she has now achieved full reintegration).

She seems more self-confident and is wanting to move forward onto this next stage of her life (said of a student in Year 11 who had been suicidal and who has now achieved full reintegration back into mainstream sixth form studies).

Interestingly, all of these comments focus on personal and social development rather than on issues of curriculum access. The comments note:

- instances of enhanced self-esteem and self-confidence;
- improved social fluency;
- enhanced self-awareness;
- some improved work habits.

In summary, these comments describe young people who are happier with themselves and with their lives and who are therefore better able to cope with the challenges and opportunities presented by mainstream schools. Although this immediate feedback is instructive, the school intends now to develop a system of following up students six months after their last formal contact, again using a related set of evaluative questions. This will provide a connected set of records from referral, through the time in which a pupil is involved with the unit, and on into life back in the mainstream, and will give staff at the unit a real sense of the long-term impact of their work.

The same school also wishes to develop means of gathering student perceptions about the long-term impact on students. At the moment, such views are gathered informally and unsystematically. Some students, for example, stay in touch with staff through visits and letters after returning to mainstream. Some of the comments which students make on leaving for mainstream are given below.

I've made loads of progress here, I think – especially getting back to school. Even though I'm going to have to go to a home tuition unit, I have had lessons at school and even been for a couple of days. I think that's good because when I first came here I was determined never to go back to school for a lesson again, let alone for a full day!

I've made loads of friends here – too many to count, I think. But I am definitely going to keep in touch with all of them because they are all really nice people and they have helped me a lot.

It has changed the way I think, though, and for the better. I've learned loads. I've learned how to trust people, learned to cry, learned to talk to people and, most importantly, I've learned about myself and my feelings.

I had to look at myself from a different angle which hasn't been easy but the help from the staff which was given to me helped me through it.

When I first came here, I had given up on school altogether. I had got more and more behind with the workload and course work and I had got to the point where I thought I could do nothing. But when I got into school here, my teacher and I started planning.

These comments provide a fascinating insight into the pupil perspective. They are important because:

- they give the staff a sense of the importance of the work they do;
- they offer an important insight into the factors that students themselves see as significant in their recoveries – making friends, learning to trust, learning to communicate, finding new ways to view themselves;
- they tell staff in the mainstream of education about some of the things that can go wrong for some learners in that context – falling behind with work, for example, and losing the capacity to be able to conceive of the possibility of catching up.

In the context of this book, these are significant insights. They show that pupils, perhaps especially those pupils who are experiencing difficulties, have a lot to tell staff about ways of improving the processes of teaching and learning and that schools who fail to take account of these perspectives risk missing a crucial source of evaluative comment. They also show that staff in mainstream and specialist contexts have a great deal to learn from one another and, arguably, that they should be working closely together on ways of aligning their service much more effectively with one another. They also show, particularly in the final comment above, the power of partnership. What gave hope to the student who had lost all faith in the possibility of achieving anything at school was not extra homework, additional tuition or reward for achievement but the act of collaboration. Involving students in shared planning can provide a sense of working together to meet the challenges of the future and this may be the most significant factor in promoting achievement.

The prime importance of collaboration on a number of fronts is also brought out in the following illustrative case study from one school's report.

Clive was admitted after approximately twelve months 'condoned truancy' from school due to excessive tics and vocal disturbances. Clive's parents were blaming the school for his problems, citing excessive bullying from peers. School staff felt that they were dealing with the matter by accepting medical notes explaining Clive's absences and sending work home for him.

Our academic assessments suggested a student of exceptional ability who was seriously underachieving. Intensive work in the classroom looked at raising his self-esteem and self-confidence through circle-time, a thinking skills programme, personal and social education and appropriate academic expectations and attainments. Much of this centred around learning to live with the immediate practical difficulties such a condition caused and finding positive alternative coping strategies.

At the same time, focused work with the family took place, encouraging them to support Clive in a positive, empowering style rather than the previous, disempowering and over-protective manner.

A reintegration programme began, supported by professional development activities with the learning support staff, the administrators and the teaching staff from the mainstream school. This was aimed at enabling a truly united front for this boy, who was not averse to using his circumstances to manipulate situations to his own advantage. Nine months on from discharge, his attendance is still excellent and grades B or C are predicted in eight subjects at GCSE.

In this case, as in so many others, the value added by the specialist provision is not strictly academic, although in this school the approach does enable many pupils to achieve good examination results. Input from staff, which included many of the strategies for enhanced pupil involvement described in this book, focused on improving the pupil's view of himself as a person and as a learner. Other strategies which contributed to a positive outcome entailed high quality collaboration between professionals from the mainstream and specialist contexts and the family. It is the 'united front' reported by staff in this vignette which appears to be one of the critical factors in securing reintegration for Clive. We suggest that this is something that colleagues from a range of professional backgrounds will need to learn to achieve more frequently in a more inclusive education system in the future.

Of course, not all the stories the project schools tell of reintegration are positive. As we reported in Chapter 2, 'Pupils as partners', Robert found himself better able to articulate his preferences as a result of being involved in this project. At the time of the project he used his newly found advocacy skills in order to negotiate a reintegration opportunity for himself. This appeared at first to be successful but, after a three-week full-time trial at the beginning of the school year, Robert expressed a desire to continue his studies at his special school and his reintegration placement was ended. This was a difficult decision for Robert to make and, in many ways, a disappointing outcome for staff who had invested a great deal of effort in preparing Robert's route back into the mainstream of education.

However, the key issue here is that Robert, in full consultation with his family and after experiencing both placements and the opportunities they offered him, made this decision for himself. Robert's school counsellor reports:

I don't see his subsequent refusal to attend mainstream as a failure. I think it proves that his new-found assertiveness and self-esteem enabled him to know what he wanted and where he wanted to be. It also gave him the confidence to state that in no uncertain terms!

Robert's decision may not have been entirely in harmony with the current political climate in education, but it was his own decision and Robert reached his conclusion from a fully informed perspective. If, as practitioners and policy-makers, we are serious about empowering pupils and students to make decisions, we must learn to accept that they may express preferences which may be at odds with our own professional perspectives.

Robert continues to make good progress at his special school. He was elected onto the school council and has campaigned successfully for a change in the school rules regarding students' use of space at breaktimes. Robert's capacity for active involvement in school affairs has therefore attained new heights. It is also worth noting that, since Robert decided not to pursue his opportunity for reintegration, four other pupils from the school have successfully returned to mainstream education, three into local primary schools and one into the secondary phase.

Impact on staff

Within the descriptions of practice in this book, we have already seen what a powerful tool the 'Involving Pupils' project has been in enabling staff to reflect on their own practice, testing new approaches and influencing the way in which the curriculum can better respond to individual needs. The following examples are derived partly from the reports of the participating schools and partly from the reflections of a group of school project coordinators who met with project leaders in the latter stages of the writing of this book in order to discuss new developments in their schools arising from their work on the 'Involving Pupils' project.

Many staff have commented upon the increased self-confidence, assertiveness and self-assurance of pupils during the work of this project. Rather than taking a defensive and negative stance with pupils who are understanding and feeling their own empowerment, staff have looked at positive and creative ways of utilising developing skills such as problem-solving and conflict resolution. The following example shows how staff in one school have increased their own confidence in pupils.

An example of Circle-Time in use most recently in the upper school has been with a behaviourally problematic Year 10 group. This particular year group have recently had difficulties relating to each other, often leading to tension and emotional outbursts that have consequently had to be dealt with by staff.

In an attempt to optimise academic achievement, the year group has been split up for most subjects, thus keeping fractious individuals apart. However, it was felt that these pupils needed the opportunity to discuss, reflect, and negotiate their behaviour together in order to develop their social skills and to try to resolve misunderstandings before they developed into conflict.

Despite a rough ride initially, with one of the teachers describing it as 'at times being like an out of control Jerry Springer show', progress is undoubtedly being made. It would be misleading to state that nearly a term later, the group were now angelic and totally unselfish in their interactions with each other, but the fact that staff are prepared to take a trial combined group to a local college on a regular basis is evidence in itself of increased confidence amongst staff of pupils' ability to socialise appropriately.

There are clear rewards here for both staff and pupils. However, without the willingness of staff to take the 'risk', the outcome would not have been so positive. This is a classic 'win–win' situation, demonstrating that staff investing confidence and trust in pupils is as important in the process of relationships in learning as pupils putting trust in staff.

Other 'win–win' situations have occurred, for example in one school where the process of target setting has enskilled staff in setting appropriate, measurable targets and helped pupils to more successfully meet their targets. In this school staff report that their ability to communicate effectively with pupils has increased considerably. The process for this school has been seen both as a staff development and personal development opportunity. Staff are better planners and communicators, and therefore better teachers.

Another school reflects on the changes that have happened in staff thinking as a result of their involvement in the project.

Teachers have also needed to develop and extend their own range of skills and capabilities. They are increasingly concerned with supervising individual or small group learning. This calls for specific skills in coordination, planning, monitoring, group structuring and dynamics, resource and personal management.

In this school, where team-teaching and mentor reflection was a focus for teachers and learning support assistants, there has been a cross-fertilisation of skills. This has led to teachers and learning support assistants identifying specific personal training needs, which relate much more closely to the needs of their pupils. One member of staff reflects, 'I never used to think about what pupils might want out of my training. It was always a personal viewpoint – a kind of self-centred approach. The project has made me rethink all of that. Pupils told us what they needed us to be able to do, and that's how I view my training needs from now on.' This member of staff is not only demonstrating that she values the views of her pupils, but also recognising that she is a learner who can be directed by them. This is a radical and, again, 'risky' approach, but one with which this member of staff was very comfortable.

In the words of one school, 'staff have begun to think about the philosophical basis of their work'. This has been evidenced in several schools, for example:

- through staff meetings where the nature of the learning programmes offered to pupils has been debated and changes made as a result;
- in the emphasis on developing and offering personal and social education opportunities to all pupils in a school where examination results have previously been considered more important;
- through the development of guidance systems which afford time to individual pupils on a weekly basis, at the cost of reorganising other areas of the curriculum;
- in the way that many schools have encouraged school councils to be more autonomous and have actively supported pupil empowerment.

In these schools staff have, again, listened closely to what pupils are saying and have made decisions, sometimes against their better judgements, to try new approaches.

There are no examples where staff express regret at trying something new.

A theme running through most reports is that of self-reflection. Teachers and support staff are rarely afforded time for reflection on their own practice due to the constraints of the curriculum and organisation of the school day. Where it has happened through the support of the 'Involving Pupils' project, practitioners have made some illuminating comments.

At the end of every session I was able to sit for thirty minutes and write notes on each student's response. I had time to check against their targets. I had time to talk with the teacher I'd just been working with. She would make constructive comments about my performance and suggest things I could try. I can't ever remember having had time to do this, and may not have time in the future, but it is incredibly powerful and I've valued it immensely.

Through the project, time has been created for joint planning and team-teaching opportunities and for critical analysis of practice, which has been invaluable.

The tutorial at the end of the day enabled me to find out how students felt about my teaching. They were very honest and always told me when something worked well. I would then try incorporating their 'best practice' into my 'best practice'.

Watching video footage of myself and my colleagues enabled us to be quite focused about the differences in each other's styles and approaches, also to the way we worked with difficult and challenging behaviours. Although you can't just copy how somebody else does it, you take the bits that you know are going to be useful in developing your own style further. Why don't we always do this?

These comments suggest that practitioners within the project have derived benefit from self-reflection, receiving the views of pupils and staff on their performance, talking with each other about practice and making adjustments and sometimes major changes to their own styles of delivery. Clearly, this is much more possible to achieve in cultures where trust, confidence and mutual support between staff and students is highly developed.

Many staff have valued the process of the 'Involving Pupils' project itself and have, themselves, felt valued by other colleagues both inside and out of their own schools and felt an increased sense of purpose and achievement. Staff have expressed these feelings in different ways.

For the staff involved the benefits have also been very positive. Meeting regularly with other project members has been rewarding and helped us to map out ideas for future work. It has enabled links to be made with other schools and contact with staff who have a common purpose.

We have all taken messages from each other. There has been a sense of camaraderie amongst project coordinators – an amazing sense of respect for each other and each other's situations. Also a will for each other's schools to be successful.

This flies in the face of the trend for competition between schools, and schools' reluctance to share their strengths and successes with others. One project coordinator observed:

There was no sense of competition – this was all about collaboration and collaborative processes. It doesn't fit with this whole drive towards performance-related pay, league tables, introspective and self-protective schools. We have been supportive of each other and have encouraged development in each other's schools. We have also been able to share some of the good practice between us, especially individual education plans, schemes of work, materials being used successfully and teaching approaches.

Other participants referred to 'having a vision', 'working with other schools', 'cross-fertilisation of ideas', 'motivation', 'reflection', 'endorsing', 'inspiring' to describe features of the collaborative aspects of the project. This illustrates the obvious sense of mutual support evident in schools involved in collaborative work. Without the focus of a 'project' it is sometimes difficult for schools to create opportunities to benefit from sharing ideas, resources and best practice. We suggest that schools should be actively seeking ways in which to support collaborative practice.

Perhaps one of the most revealing observations made by a project coordinator about the processes of being involved in the project concerned that of positive modelling. He suggested that the LEA had supported the project, that the project leaders had empowered school staff, who had created processes to empower pupils. There is clear evidence in this book that not only has there been 'top down' support for the work of schools, but also 'bottom up' motivation to impact on practice.

Impact on the curriculum

In several schools involved in developing thinking skills, evaluation led to reflections about the changes occurring in curriculum planning and delivery. Some of these were concentrated on a narrow range of subjects, some on the whole school. They nevertheless all point to the need for more highly developed roles in the curriculum for the teaching of thinking skills and key skills. The revised *National Curriculum* (DfEE/QCA 1999) begins to address the problem, although it remains to be seen how much more flexibility in the organisation and delivery of the curriculum will be offered to schools.

In its final report, one school observes:

The teaching of thinking skills is now an entitlement within the personal and social education curriculum. Further development within personal and social education will involve the dissemination of results and materials to staff involved in core subjects. Teachers will then be able to decide if the thinking skills approach is an alternative way of approaching difficult subject matter.

The sense of a 'questioning' school is exemplified by this positive, proactive statement, which assumes already that alternative approaches to curriculum development are going to be received without threat by other staff in the school.

Another school, in evaluating the effectiveness of one thinking skills programme, leads on to comments about how the work is likely to impact on development in a whole-school context.

The Top Ten Tactics *proved to be a good starting point for group discussion, providing materials which are clear and concise and requiring no extra preparation by the teacher. Access to the materials and tasks required much more teacher direction and prompting than had been anticipated and a great deal of careful explanation preceded tasks.*

The outcome of the project has been to confirm that the development of student self-esteem and social skills (including social language) should be a priority. The way forward will require an evaluation of the pastoral curriculum, staff training (mentoring, Circle-Time), the setting up of a student council and a review of the opportunities available to students in terms of equality.

Again, there is a sense of determination and expectation in the way intentions are expressed.

One school had started with the premise that their learning programmes did not always match the needs of the students. In their evaluation comments, a sense of achievement is evident, reflecting the high sense of student participation in effecting these changes:

- *the identified need for a change of focus and direction has become a reality;*
- *this change of direction involved pupils' views and suggestions at all stages and so is more likely to succeed;*
- *a thinking skills programme relevant to the particular needs of young people has been developed;*
- *the programme is now more relevant to the current client group needs;*
- *an outreach programme has been developed and permanent funding has recently been secured to support its development in the future;*
- *the assessment process has been improved;*
- *curriculum content relates more specifically to skills required for successful reintegration.*

Further challenges and opportunities are also articulated:

- *to extend the evaluation of the effectiveness of the service by increasing the time span to a six-month audit;*
- *to develop the nationally accredited, self-directed ASDAN programme for all young people, focusing on key skills, independent learning and target setting;*
- *to formalise the philosophical basis of work in the classroom.*

We believe we operate through a cognitive behavioural approach. We are aware that most, if not all, of our young people will hold irrational, illogical and distorted beliefs, attitudes and expectations about themselves and others. They are likely to think unduly negatively about their abilities, their self-image and their future prospects, particularly in comparison to their peers.

We therefore aim to help the young people identify and correct their illogical thinking about themselves and others and encourage them to identify and focus on positive aspects of themselves. This would seem to fit the criteria of such cognitive interventions as problem-solving therapy and we will be exploring this further.

The consideration of curricular change does not, however, stop here. Staff have also considered some implications for mainstream schools.

- *Empowered young people who have gained confidence to speak out are not always welcome in mainstream schools!*
- *Similarly, schools who place a strong emphasis on the curriculum and exam results are unlikely to acknowledge the skills learnt through our structure.*
- *Hopefully, with the introduction of specific behaviour support programmes both nationally and locally, mainstream schools are being encouraged to empower and involve pupils in their approaches to individual, group and whole-school management of behaviour. Many of the suggested approaches are evidenced in the work of special schools and units and as such may be a source of advice and guidance to mainstream schools.*

These perceptive comments serve only to strengthen the notion of increased collaboration between the specialist and mainstream sectors expressed in the previous section.

Another school reports change to its curriculum as a result of the project.

We are now developing Promoting Alternative Thinking Strategies (PATHS) as part of the learning programme. Once a week in the lower school a lesson is dedicated to this project, originally developed by Helen Reed of the National Deaf Children's Society (NDCS) for use with pupils with hearing impairments in order to help them understand and explore their emotions. It has been effectively adapted at the school to be used with hearing pupils.

In these lessons pupils are taught the meaning of emotional vocabulary, e.g. sad, happy, jealous, etc., and how to control behaviour appropriately. Pupils are taught that all feelings are fine, but that the associated behaviour with some of these feelings is not (e.g. it is okay to be angry, but not to kick the cat!). It is important that pupils are aware that adults have feelings too and they are encouraged to express them rather than mask them.

In each lesson a child is chosen by lot to be the special helper for the teacher and at the end of the lesson, everyone in the class including any adults involved give a compliment to that child. These compliments are typed up and sent home at the end of the day.

One of the emphases of the project is to encourage problem-solving together, after equipping children with the language they need to discuss the issues raised. The pupils are encouraged to bring what they perceive to be problems to the lesson and then are given the opportunity to try to come up with some solutions of their own, in small groups.

Although still in its infancy, the project is considered to be having a marked impact on how conflicts are resolved with the pupils involved.

Although the introduction of PATHS in this school has shown rapid rewards, there remain tensions to do with how schools can acknowledge, and take account of, pupil perspectives on curriculum development, when the National Curriculum (although more flexible) is still highly prescriptive.

Issues in school development

We have described some significant developments in schools as a result of the work of the 'Involving Pupils' project. These include:

- the setting up of school councils;
- reviews of, and adaptations to, the curriculum;
- changes in the process of reintegrating pupils into mainstream provision;
- developments in target setting, tracking and review;
- changes to teaching and learning styles and approaches, for example the introduction of Circle-Time, team-teaching, mentoring, individual action planning.

The common factor in all the above developments is that of collaboration between:

- pupils and their peers;
- pupils and staff;
- pupils and senior managers;
- staff and senior managers.

In all cases, changes have been made as a result of pupils and staff working together, furthered by support from senior management teams. Collaboration demands trust, mutual support, confidence and determination, examples of which are clearly seen in the reports of participating schools and exemplified by one school in the following statement:

perhaps the photographs of the [school] council next to those of the staff in the entrance hall best epitomises the message they wish to communicate to the school community: 'In this school, pupils have a voice that is listened to'.

Project coordinators agreed that school developments were initiated largely through the teaching and learning process and, because of the nature of the project, driven by pupil and student views. One coordinator states that 'the effect of what was happening in classrooms influenced wider school developments'.

In some schools, the influence of the project was even wider still. At more than one school, as a result of the gradual changes in special educational needs policy and provision, the range of pupils' difficulties has become increasingly diverse. Therefore staff have developed their skills to teach pupils whose needs present them with different challenges. Special schools are starting to work more closely with local mainstream schools to share expertise, to problem-solve together, to raise awareness and promote good practice. An example of this in one school is the way in which the deputy head teacher has been closely involved in the staff development programme of a local primary school, sharing her expertise in the use of circle-time, as well as working to help the school meet the needs of pupils with special educational needs. The work of another school has led to a major inclusion initiative with a local mainstream secondary school, where staff from the special school are actively supporting students and also mainstream staff in learning how to meet a wider range of needs. These school developments reflect the DfEE's (1998) intentions that specialist centres should be changing and adapting their roles in order to further support inclusive practices in mainstream schools.

One school, in its final report, concludes:

The challenge of the future makes it even more necessary to actively develop those skills that will enable pupils to make choices, negotiate, find solutions, share ideas and communicate effectively.

Whether pupils are to remain at this special school or to continue their education in a mainstream setting, we need to ensure they have a clear understanding of what it is they need to learn, and how they can learn best.

More than ever before, we need to give pupils formal and informal opportunities to interact with adults so that we can receive pupil perspectives in order to make them active participants in the school culture.

The future challenge for special schools requires that pupils and students are even more prepared for moving into mainstream situations. This may involve the need to reframe the curriculum offered in special schools in order that there is a more acceptable balance between the requirements of the National Curriculum and the need to teach pupils the wide range of personal, social, communication and study skills required to survive and flourish in the mainstream.

During a meeting held to gather the views of some of the project coordinators on the draft of this book, there were opportunities for colleagues to reflect further on their participation. One coordinator said, 'being close to school development you don't always appreciate some of the changes that have happened. The work on the project has become embedded in the culture of school – you come to expect it . . . that was why it was so valuable being part of project.' He said that until he had read the document he had forgotten how far they had come. This is a reflection not only on the success of the *process* of being involved in the project but also on the success of the school in internalising the developments and changing and adapting some of its systems, processes and practices. Other schools commented similarly that, rather than having a major impact on school development, the project had predominantly influenced practice, resulting in staff and pupils who felt empowered as agents of change. All schools recognised and acknowledged that there have been changes in school culture. Although these are extremely difficult to define, they are to do with the way learners build respect for other learners through communicating, listening and responding, working on new ways of relating to each other in learning situations and on gaining skills in articulating views, opinions, needs, wishes and aspirations.

In all schools, senior management teams have been influenced by the work undertaken during the project. In some schools the work fed directly into school development planning in a variety of ways, for example instigating reviews of the curriculum, school organisation, training and development programmes and policies on behaviour, pupil complaints, guidance and support. In one school the project led to additional personnel being employed for counselling and guidance, in three others there were changes in the way that staff were deployed. In the 'Practice' chapters we show evidence of the impact of some schools on policy review and development.

The focus for the project in each school was originally linked to some element of school development. In each of the schools the work was evolutionary and grew in momentum. Like all school development initiatives, there was a process involved, with which we are familiar in school development planning. Targets or goals were set, programmes or tasks implemented, reviewed, evaluated and new targets set. The project therefore modelled good practice in the process of the school development cycle. It is further encouraging that the data gathered on the effectiveness of projects undertaken in all the schools has impacted on further school development, particularly in the areas of curriculum design and innovation and staff development.

Significantly, many of the project staff were not senior managers and, as such, may not have had firsthand experience of the school development cycle. Several staff commented that they had become more skilled in tracking processes – 'becoming more efficient and effective in planning and carrying out projects, looking for evidence, recording it and presenting it', as one project coordinator explained. There are two benefits here. One in the personal development and enskilling of classroom practitioners in the cycle of target setting and review, which leads to the second – the benefit for schools in harnessing these skills at management and classroom level, giving schools higher potential to effect meaningful and effective improvement.

Reflections on data-gathering methods

Schools in the project identified improved data management as one of the positive outcomes of participating. Using data for tracking and evaluating changes was demonstrated in all schools. Some also reported becoming more efficient and effective in planning and carrying out projects.

Thinking ahead about data collection and how it might be used has been highlighted as a message for the future. For example, at one school, gathering pupil perception data proved highly influential in pinpointing the need for change and stimulating action. However by the end of the project the main target group of pupils had left the school. Therefore it was not possible to repeat the data collection to give evidence of change. Staff expressed regret at targeting Year 9/10 groups for what could have provided valuable baseline data. Had they targeted Year 7 groups, follow up data could have been collected for comparison with baseline data during the life of the project. Nevertheless it is important to recognise the pragmatic reasons for choices such as this. The year groups concerned were those where there had been much staff concern. Choosing a younger group primarily for research purposes would have been an inappropriate priority. As Robson (1993) helpfully reassures us, research in the 'real world' is about 'seeking to say something sensible about a complex, relatively poorly controlled and generally "messy" situation'. Planning how to use data before gathering it is essential but caution should be given to avoid data management leading professional judgement. Otherwise we are in danger of valuing what can be measured rather than measuring what we value.

Staff at another school have developed interview schedules as a key tool for gathering students' views of new teaching programmes. Their experience of obtaining limited responses to written questionnaires led them to using questionnaire formats as prompts in structured interviews (Cohen and Manion 1994). Effectively, these are spoken questionnaires with responses recorded by the interviewer. For pupils with low self-esteem or literacy difficulties this removes a considerable barrier and raises motivation to participate. Using a prepared format rather than open-ended questioning also reduces potential anxiety about the purpose of the interview and makes it clear that students' views are being collected as part of a formal process of reviewing the curriculum. This raises the status of the process and demonstrates the value placed on the student voice.

At the same school, seeking feedback in order to evaluate provision for individual students has been a feature of practice for some while. This involves sending questionnaires to students' new schools. Staff are now in the process of extending this to seek comments from students themselves. Informal feedback is already received in the form of letters and contact on follow-up visits. The implications of their data-gathering are described above in 'Implications for reintegration and inclusion'.

In several schools, questionnaires proved a valuable source of data and evidence, leading to clear issues for action. Evidence was gathered in this way from pupils through questionnaires delivered as part of teaching and learning sessions, from staff in confidential questionnaires and from parents through questionnaires sent to parents with Annual Reviews, annual reports and IEPs. The use of parent questionnaires in one school is now embedded within the processes of monitoring, evaluation and review.

Two schools used video footage to good effect in order to help staff and pupils reflect on their practice. The use of video is not so much to do with what is recorded but with the issues and questions which arise from observing practice (Tilstone 1998). Video is a powerful way to disseminate good practice and effective ways of evaluating the quality of practice. As in real life, observers will draw different conclusions, make different links and ask different questions.

CHAPTER 6

Conclusions and Audit Check

Introduction

In the opening chapter of this book we set out three major themes, which seemed to us to reflect the wide scope of the 'Involving Pupils' project. These were:

- pupil empowerment and enhanced self-esteem;
- impact on school ethos and culture;
- promoting inclusion.

We argued that affording respect to learners and enhancing self-esteem are important values in education; that self-esteem is likely to be raised more effectively where pupils are involved as active participants in their own learning. We suggested that pupils' views should be listened to carefully and taken seriously by teachers and other professionals. In order to listen to pupils and respond to their needs more effectively, we outlined the need for staff in schools to reflect on their own practice and become more flexible in their approaches to teaching and learning. We stressed the advantages of a culture of collaboration in moving towards more inclusive practices, both within individual schools and between neighbouring schools. We asserted that more flexible approaches to the delivery of the curriculum and methods of gathering individual pupil views would support the process of schools becoming more inclusive. We emphasised that the involvement of pupils in practice concerned the culture and ethos of the whole school and that the responsibility for listening and responding to pupils' needs belonged to all of us.

In the previous chapter, 'Evaluation and Implications', we have reflected and commented upon these three themes from a range of perspectives. In this chapter we summarise the main findings of the 'Involving Pupils' project, further reflecting the above themes.

Summary and commentary

In the following set of paired ideas, we present a summary of evidence from the 'Involving Pupils' project together with some more forward-looking, speculative comment. In each case our tentative conclusions based on the small-scale, but illustrative, set of case studies we have offered in this book are given first as bullet points. We then offer our own suggestions for follow-up or for the proposed wider application of ideas, which we acknowledge to go beyond the immediate outcomes of the 'Involving Pupils' project itself. These are presented in italics.

- Involvement in target setting, monitoring progress and review leads to pupils becoming more effective learners.

Further research is needed in order to explore this tentative conclusion on a wider basis and among pupils with a range of individual needs.

- The learners who participated in the 'Involving Pupils' project responded positively to support designed to help them to develop the skills necessary to maximise involvement in their own learning.

Arguably these skills should be:

- *made explicit in curriculum planning;*
- *directly taught to all learners;*
- *embedded into schemes of work for the full range of subjects;*
- *targeted in pupils' individual education plans.*

- Learning how to learn is empowering for learners and has a positive impact upon self-esteem and the development of the whole individual.

Although we have demonstrated this to be the case specifically and dramatically for pupils with special educational needs, all schools should create opportunities for all pupils to work on improving their own learning and performance and to develop thinking skills.

- Holding tutorials and building new forms of relationship based on negotiation between teachers and learners has been shown to influence pupil behaviour, attitude and motivation to learn in positive ways.

Staff need to explore new forms of relationship with learners which are characterised by a shift in control:

- *from didactic towards more facilitative styles;*
- *from instruction towards mentoring.*

- The ability of members of staff to set realistic achievable targets for learning improves when they work in partnership with pupils.

Staff should work with pupils on the setting of targets across the age range and across the spectrum of achievement, since pupil involvement helps staff to come to an enriched understanding of the power of targets.

- The staff who became involved in the 'Involving Pupils' project swiftly identified a need to be supported in developing the skills necessary for negotiating effectively with pupils.

Staff in all educational contexts should be offered access to professional development opportunities focused on learning to listen to the pupil perspective – these skills in active listening, attending to the whole pupil, negotiation and shared action planning could be loosely described as counselling skills.

- The staff who participated in the 'Involving Pupils' project found their attitudes and their practice changing in significant ways.

In order to develop the confidence to enable them to reframe their approaches to teaching and learning, staff should be supported in the process of committing themselves to self-review and reflective practice.

- Significant changes in the practice of individual members of staff have implications for whole-school development.

Schools should commit themselves to a constant cycle of review and revision of policy and practice in which the perspectives of all members of the school community, including pupils and members of staff at all levels, are valued.

- Staff development and pupil mentoring demand time and investment.

School development plans should show resources being allocated to promoting pupil involvement and school managers must seek out and protect funding in support of the development of this dimension in teaching and learning.

- Schools in the 'Involving Pupils' project developed a view of the curriculum as a flexible entity which is increasingly and appropriately focused on cross-curricular issues including key skills, thinking skills and the personal and social development of the whole pupil.

Time in the school week should be allocated to taught courses in personal and social education and teaching thinking skills as well as for planning and review meetings with tutors and mentors.

- Many important aspects of pupil progress and achievement cannot be measured using standard measures of academic attainment.

Measures of pupil outcomes should be expanded to encompass issues like:

- *enhanced pupil self-esteem;*
- *evidence of greater pupil empowerment;*
- *pupils acting as effective advocates for their own points of view both individually, for example in dialogue with a member of school staff or an employer, and in group contexts, for example in school councils or lobby groups.*

- Pupils are eminently well-equipped to make critical and positive suggestions for revised policy and practice through initiatives like Circle-Time and school councils.

School communities should create opportunities for pupils to come together to express shared views and perceptions. School communities should learn to hear these views and perspectives and act upon them.

- Pupils generate high-quality data, both individually and collectively, which schools ignore at their peril.

Evidence of school effectiveness should include measures which make use of pupil perspectives.

- Working together is powerful and important.

Collaboration should be encouraged between:

- *pupils and other pupils;*
- *staff and pupils;*
- *staff and other adults, professionals and parents;*
- *schools and other agencies and institutions, including other schools.*

- High quality interpersonal processes, between staff and pupils; pupils and other pupils; staff and parents; and within the staff group, are an important characteristic of improving schools.

School structures and procedures should support, rather than dominating or compromising, sophisticated forms of interaction between all members of the school community.

- In order to foster innovative work, it may be important to give it the status of being 'a project'. Such a project may have a self-identified focus, but requires clearly defined tasks with support and guidance from project leaders and senior managers.

More funding should be made available to support such initiatives which combine 'bottom up' motivation with 'top down' facilitation.

Audit checklist

In Chapter 1 we set out a range of characteristics that we would expect to be common to schools who are involving pupils effectively in practice. The 'Practice' chapters have described a wide range of approaches to increasing pupil involvement and Chapter 5, 'Evaluation and Implications', has described the positive outcomes and the issues arising from the work of project schools. The above 'Summary and commentary' section has focused main findings and offered suggestions for further inquiry.

We now offer a checklist of the characteristics of schools which might be said to be involving pupils effectively. Colleagues might like to use this list in order to:

- stimulate debate among staff, pupils and parents;
- undertake an audit of policy and/or practice in their own schools.

We do not suggest that this is an exhaustive list but we do hope it is at least thought-provoking and challenging.

Involving Pupils in Practice Checklist

Do staff and pupils engage in dialogue about teaching and learning?

- Do staff make use of a wide range of informal opportunities to enter into a dialogue with pupils about their learning?
- Is time set aside for staff and pupils to negotiate targets for learning; review progress; agree revised targets?
- Are pupils with statements of special educational needs actively and meaningfully involved in the Annual Review process?
- Do staff constantly seek to expand pupils' opportunities to express their views, needs, interests, choices, preferences and decisions through the use of conventional, augmentative and alternative modes of communication?
- Do staff make every effort to develop ways in which pupils with special educational needs can be actively involved as participants in formal meetings, such as those held as part of the processes of Annual Review and Annual Reporting?
- Are targets for improving pupils' own learning and performance included in IEPs where appropriate?
- Do staff receive training in active listening, counselling, conducting tutorials, mentoring skills?

Do staff actively promote pupils' capacity to think?

- Are there lessons dedicated to the direct teaching of thinking skills, study skills and skills for learning?
- Do staff review schemes of work for all subjects in order to identify opportunities for developing key skills and thinking skills?
- Are key skills, for example problem-solving skills and skills for learning, actively promoted in a range of contexts across the curriculum?
- Are pupils encouraged to create formal and informal 'buddying', peer tutoring, circles of friends and mentoring relationships focused on personal and social skills, positive behaviour, survival strategies and teaching and learning?

Do pupils put forward their own ideas?

- Do representatives from the student council play an active role in the selection of staff?
- Do pupils act as agents of control in decision-making processes at a school development level?
- Are pupils involved in developing:

- codes of conduct for classroom behaviour and discipline
- whole-school approaches to policy and practice in behaviour management
- policy in relation to bullying
- mentoring relationships between individual pupils with difficult behaviours?

- Do pupils participate in the process of institutional development at a whole-school level, for example by participating in school council meetings?

Do staff attend to pupil views and perspectives?

- Are pupil perspectives discussed as a regular item on the agenda for staff meetings, senior management team meetings and governing body meetings?
- Do staff encourage, facilitate and make constructive responses to ideas and initiatives that are put forward by pupils?
- Do staff engage pupils in constructive debate about ideas and initiatives put forward by other pupils?
- Do staff take account of parent/carer, family and enablers' interpretations of pupils' views and perspectives?
- Do staff take account of other agencies' interpretations of pupils' views and perspectives, for example health, social services, the voluntary sector?

Do governors attend to pupil views and perspectives?

- Does the governing body seek to elect or co-opt representation from individuals with learning and/or other disabilities in the local community?
- Do members of the governing body respond positively to invitations to attend and participate in school council meetings?
- Are there 'link' governors who have a brief to listen regularly to the views of pupils and students, either formally or informally?
- Does the governing body receive and respond constructively to reports from the school council and/or reports about the work of the school council?

Do senior managers attend to pupil views and perspectives?

- Does the school articulate clearly its values about pupil involvement?
- Do senior managers regularly review the relationship between stated policy and practice?
- Do senior managers ensure that lines of communication in the school community remain open?
- Do senior managers demonstrate a commitment to hearing the views of all members of the school community, including the perspectives of pupils?
- Do senior managers provide a model of respecting and responding to the views of other members of the school community?
- Are pupils' views fed back to senior managers and governors through a range of approaches to the exchange of information between staff, for example regular

meetings with mid-day supervisory assistants, learning support assistants, staff personal and professional development meetings etc?

Do school systems and procedures take account of pupil perspectives?

- Does the school have pupil support, guidance, suggestions and complaints procedures which are readily available, understood and used, when necessary, by pupils?
- Does the school use a range of approaches for gathering pupils' views and perceptions, for example by questionnaire, interviews, Circle-Time reports?
- Is data gathered through pupil questionnaires, interviews and used in the development of
  - curriculum content (what pupils are taught)
  - effective pedagogy (how pupils are taught)
  - an improved school environment
  - enhanced resources
  - expanded opportunities
  - an improved climate for learning?

- Are pupils' comments and judgements about their school experiences listened to, valued and, where appropriate, acted upon?
- Are pupils' views channelled into the school development process via Circle-Time, personal and social education lessons, tutorials, individual review or action planning meetings?
- Does the school development plan contain targets which reflect priorities identified by pupils and students?
- Are staff encouraged to be reflective practitioners, re-evaluating their work in the light of pupil perspectives and entering into critical friendships with colleagues?

Concluding comments

We hope that the work of schools participating in the 'Involving Pupils' project and the authors' commentary have prompted readers to reflect on some of their own needs, issues and priorities and that the work described in this book will help to make a further impact on practice. If readers wish to follow up any aspects of work undertaken in the participating schools, full addresses, telephone/fax numbers and contacts are supplied in the 'Participating Schools' section following this chapter.

Resources

The following resources are listed by title.

Adolescent Coping Scale. (Frydenberg, E. and Lewis, R.) Australian Council for Educational Research (ACER) (1993).

British Picture Vocabulary Scale. (Dunn, L. M., Whetton, C. and Pintilie, D.), NFER Nelson (1982).

Dynamic Standard Setting System. (Kendal, H.) 'Quality Patient Care: the Dynamic Standard Setting System'. Royal College of Nursing (1990).

Macmillan Reading Test. Macmillan Education (1985).

NFER Comprehension Test. NFER Nelson (1990).

NFER Reading Test. NFER Nelson (1990).

Profile of Maths Skills. Nelson (1979).

Quality Circle Time. (Mosley, J.) Learning Development Aids, Wisbech (1996).

Ravens Matrices. (Raven, J., Raven, J. C. and Court, J. H.) Oxford Psychologists Press (1988).

Richmond Test of Basic Skills. (Heironymous, A. N., Linquist, E. F. and France, N.) London (1981).

Reading-Miscue Analysis. From *Neale Analysis Reading Aloud Test.* NFER Nelson (1990).

Turn Your School Around. (Mosley, J.) Learning Development Aids, Wisbech (1993).

Thinking skills resources, including some brief summaries of materials referred to in Chapter 3

CoRT Thinking Skills. (de Bono, E.) Direct Educational Services (1974). Address: CIP Ltd, 10 Cavendish Road, Oxford OX2 TTW.

Summary
A very flexible course designed for stimulating and organising children's and adults' thinking. CoRT enables learners to view a problem from a variety of different angles and perspectives. The subject matter is based on real-life contexts. Easy to use alongside other thinking skills programmes.

The Dynamic Assessment of Retarded Performers: The Learning Potential Assessment Device, Theory, Instruments and Techniques. (Feuerstein, R.) University Park Press, Baltimore (1979).

Summary
The LPAD is a set of instruments for measuring cognitive skills and visual perception. The instruments are closely linked to the IE materials and will form a baseline assessment for designing an appropriate thinking skills programme.

Instrumental Enrichment: an intervention program for cognitive modifiability. (Feuerstein, R., Rand, Y., Hoffman, M. B. and Miller, R.) University Park Press, Baltimore (1980). Address: Scott, Foresman and Company, Lifelong Learning Division, 1900 East Lake Avenue, Glenview, IL 60025, USA.

Summary

IE is based on the premise that it is possible to teach children the cognitive skills which are deficient through lack of cultural stimuli. The materials are structured in modules, supported by progressive worksheets which are described as 'content-free'. Modules cover skills such as 'Orientation in Space', 'Organisation of dots', 'Comparisons', 'Instructions'. The teacher is seen as a 'mediator' and assists pupils to 'bridge' between the IE materials and other learning areas. People must be trained in order to teach IE.

Somerset Thinking Skills Course. (Blagg, N., Ballinger, M., Gardner, R., Petty, M. and Williams, G.) Blackwell/Somerset County Council, Oxford (1988). Address: Nigel Blagg Associates, Chartered Psychologists, Grove House, 39 Staplegrove Road, Taunton, Somerset TA1 1DG.

Summary

STSC contains many of the elements of IE in a more stylish and updated context. Each of the four modules focuses on a distinctive element of cognitive development; for example, Module 1 'Foundations for Problem-Solving' presents a number of tasks to promote lateral and connective thinking. Activities are described in three categories as 'stimulus' (provoking discussion), 'artificial' (requiring abstract connections) and 'naturalistic' (more familiar settings). The materials are interchangeable and contain clear directions to users.

Think Talk Connect. (Link, F.) University Park Press, Baltimore (1988).

Summary

Similar to IE in its structure and the role of the teacher as 'mediator' in learning experiences, and to de Bono (CoRT) in that it encourages expansive thinking. Students look at patterns, words, objects and sometimes combinations of these and talk about what they see. They are then asked to make links between these. Students practise verbal reasoning in verifying their responses, none of which are right or wrong.

Top Ten Thinking Tactics. (Lake, M. and Needham, M.) Questions: Birmingham (1990). Address: The Questions Publishing Company, 27 Frederick Street, Hockley, Birmingham B1 3HH.

Summary

A well-presented and easily accessible programme, with clear instructions to teachers for delivery and extension work, related to other areas of the curriculum and with well-designed materials. Mike Lake has worked extensively on cross-referencing skills in the *Top Ten Thinking Tactics* to the *National Curriculum*. The programme can be used as a whole course, or dipped into to suit individual or group requirements and covers skills such as 'pinpointing the problem', 'systematic search', 'comparing and contrasting', 'using several sources'.

Addresses for other major resources referred to in this book

Promoting Alternative Thinking Strategies (PATHS)
National Deaf Children's Society (NDCS)
15 Dufferin Street, London EC1Y 8UR.

Skills for Adolescence
Tacade
Furness House, Trafford Road, Salford, Manchester M5 2XJ.

Solution Focused Brief Therapy
Brief Therapy Practice
4d Shirland Mews, London W9 3DYY.

Participating Schools – Address and contacts

The Edith Borthwick School
Fennes Road, Church Street, Bocking, Braintree, Essex CM7 5LA.
Tel/Fax: 01376 326436.
Contact: Ian Boatman.

Cedar Hall School
Hart Road, Thundersley, Benfleet, Essex SS7 3UQ.
Tel: 01268 774723 Fax: 01268 776604.
Contact: Nic Maxwell.

The Hayward School
Maltese Road, Chelmsford, Essex CM1 2PA.
Tel: 01245 258667 Fax: 01245 347126.
Contact: Jude Ragan.

The Heath School
Winstree Road, Stanway, Colchester, Essex CO3 5QE.
Tel: 01206 571379 Fax: 01206 578591.
Contact: Steve Whitfield.

Longview Adolescent Unit
216 Turner Road, Colchester, Essex CO4 5JR.
Tel: 01206 228745 Fax: 01206 843702.
Contact: Carol Kirk.

Market Field School
School Road, Elmstead Market, Colchester, Essex CO7 7ET.
Tel: 01206 825195 Fax: 01206 825234.
Contact: Jude Jelly, Dave Musselwhite.

Priory School
Burr Hill Chase, Prittlewell, Southend-on-Sea, Essex SS2 6PE.
Tel: 01702 347490 Fax: 01702 432164.
Contact: Steve Sibson.

Examining bodies and certification referred to in the text

Associated Examining Board (AEB) Certificates in English, mathematics.

Award Scheme Development and Accreditation Network (ASDAN) Youth Award Scheme and Key Skills Award.

Basic Food Hygiene Certificate.

Certificate of Achievement (CoA).

Certificate of Learning and Achievement in Information Technology (CLAIT).

Edexcel Certificate of Competence (Information and Communication Technology).

English Speaking Board.

General Certificate of Secondary Education (GCSE).

Royal Society of Arts (RSA) Accredited Learning for Life (ALL).

Royal Society of Arts (RSA) English and mathematics, National Skills Profiles.

St John Ambulance First Aid Certificate.

Appendices

Thinking Skills

By using thinking skills pupils can focus on . . . learning how to learn. The following thinking skills complement the key skills and are embedded in the National Curriculum:

- **information-processing skills**

  - enable pupils to locate and collect relevant information; sort, classify, sequence, compare and contrast; analyse whole/part relationships

- **reasoning skills**

  - enable pupils to give reasons for opinions and actions; draw inferences; make deductions; explain what they think; make informed judgements and decisions

- **enquiry skills**

  - enable pupils to ask questions; pose and define problems; plan what to do; plan research; predict outcomes; anticipate consequences; test conclusions; improve ideas

- **creative thinking skills**

  - enable pupils to generate and extend ideas; suggest hypotheses; apply imagination; look for alternative outcomes

- **evaluation skills**

  - enable pupils to evaluate information; judge the value of what they read, hear, do; develop criteria for judging value of own and others' work or ideas; have confidence in judgements

QCA/DfEE (1999) *The National Curriculum.* London: DfEE/QCA.

Key Skills

Six skill areas are described as key skills because they help learners to improve their learning and performance in education, work and life. These key skills are embedded in the National Curriculum:

- ## communication

  - includes speaking, listening, reading and writing: speaking to different audiences; listening, understanding and responding to others; participating in group discussion; reading a range of texts; reflecting on what is read; writing for a range of purposes; analysing own and others' writing – opportunities for developing this key skill are provided through English in particular and through pupils' use of language across the curriculum

- ## application of number

  - includes mental calculation skills and ability to apply them in a variety of contexts: understanding and use of mathematical language related to numbers and calculations; processing data; solving problems; explaining reasoning – opportunities for developing this key skill are explicit in maths, but pupils need to be able to apply calculation skills and understanding of number in other National Curriculum subjects and to real-life situations

- ## information technology

  - includes ability to use a range of information sources and ICT tools: inquiry and decision-making skills; information processing and creative thinking skills; ability to review, modify and evaluate work – opportunities for developing this key skill are provided through subject of ICT and through use of ICT across the curriculum

QCA/DfEE (1999) *The National Curriculum.* London: DfEE/QCA.

Key Skills

- ## working with others

  – includes ability to contribute to small-group and whole-class discussion and to work with others to meet a challenge: pupils should develop social skills and growing awareness and understanding of others' needs – all subjects to provide opportunities for pupils to cooperate and work with others in formal and informal settings

- ## improving own learning and performance

  – involves reflecting on and critically evaluating their work and what they have learnt: pupils need to be able to identify purposes of learning, reflect on processes of learning, assess progress in learning, identify obstacles or problems, plan ways to improve – all subjects provide opportunities to review work and discuss ways to improve learning

- ## problem-solving

  – involves developing skills and strategies to solve problems in learning and in life: identifying and understanding a problem, planning ways to solve a problem, monitoring progress in tackling a problem, reviewing solutions to problems – all subjects provide opportunities to respond to the challenge of problems

QCA/DfEE (1999) *The National Curriculum.* London: DfEE/QCA.

Appendix 2

<u>MY ACTION PLAN</u>

<u>What am I like now?</u>	<u>What do I want to achieve?</u>

My Target(s):

<u>What will I do in order to achieve my target?</u>

<u>How will I know when I have succeeded?</u>	<u>What evidence will I show others in order to share in my success?</u>

<u>EVALUATION</u>

I have been working on my target for .... weeks. I feel ....
....
....

I feel I   need   don't need   more time to work on my target.

Signed.................................. (pupil)   Date...............................

NAME		DOB		DATE TARGETS SET		REVIEW DATE
STRENGTHS				AREAS FOR DEVELOPMENT		
TARGET	SUPPORT STRATEGIES			SUCCESS CRITERIA		EVALUATION/ REVIEW
1.						
2.						
3.						
PARENTAL COMMENTS				PUPIL COMMENTS		

Appendix 4

Annual Review: Pupil Views

This is a chance for you to say what you feel about your school and learning. Please tell us as much as you can. An adult or friend can help you if you wish.

A: Last year at school
What things did you most like doing?

What did you do best?

What improvements did you make?

What helped you to learn or get on better?

What things did you not like doing?

What things did you find difficult?

B: Next year at school
What things do you want to do better?

What things do you need help with?

Are you worried about anything?
If so, what?

Would you like to talk to anyone else?   If so, who?

Signed: Helped by: Date:

Section 2: Pupil's View

Do you like coming to school?	yes	no
What do you like to do best at school?		
What else do you like to do at school?		
What do you need help with at school?		
What do you not like at school?		
Are you happy at school?	yes	no
Did you write this form on your own or with help? on my own/with help (please ring)	If you had help give the person's name here:	Signed

Appendix 6

MY IEP ACTION PLAN, DATE:

The target from my Statement of Special Educational Needs or Annual Review I am focusing on is: (if this is relevant)

1)

2)

3)

My target(s): S M A R T	
1)	What am I like now? 0------------------5------------ ------10 What do I want to achieve? 0------------------5------------------10
2)	What am I like now? 0------------------5------------------10 What do I want to achieve? 0------------------5------------------10
3)	What am I like now? 0------------------5------------------10 What do I want to achieve? 0------------------5------------------10

What will I do in order to achieve my target?
1)

2)

3)

Evaluation

I have been working on my targets for .... weeks.

Percentage achieved.............. I feel I   need   don't need   more time on target 1.

Percentage achieved.............. I feel I   need   don't need   more time on target 2.

Percentage achieved.............. I feel I   need   don't need   more time on target 3.

Signed ....(pupil and staff member)   Date..............

MY IEP ACTION PLAN, DATE: October 1998

The target from my Statement of Special Educational Needs or Annual Review I am focusing on is: (if this is relevant)

1) To extend my concentration and attention span; to remain in class.

2) To learn the boundaries of acceptable behaviour, including developing strategies for regulating my need for adult attention.

3) To take more personal responsibility.

My target(s): S M A R T	
1) To ignore hurtful name calling, so that I stay in class.	What am I like now? 0-------------*----5-----------------10 What do I want to achieve? 0------------------5------*----------10
2) To accept the decisions of the teacher so that I stay in class.	What am I like now? 0--------------*---5-----------------10 What do I want to achieve? 0------------------5------*----------10
3) To be ready for breakfast when the bell is rung.	What am I like now? 0------------------5*----------------10 What do I want to achieve? 0------------------5---------------*10

What will I do in order to achieve my target?
1) I will try to ignore hurtful comments, if they get too much for me I shall tell the teacher, so that they can deal with it.

2) I will try to listen carefully to everything the teacher has to say and accept this without walking out of class.

3) I will get up straight away when asked to in order to be in the shower on time.

Evaluation

I have been working on my targets for ...6... weeks.

Percentage achieved.........65... I feel I   _**need**_   don't need   more time on target 1.

Percentage achieved.........50... I feel I   _**need**_   don't need   more time on target 2.

Percentage achieved........100... I feel I   need   _**don't need**_   more time on target 3.

Signed ....(pupil and staff member)   Date...............

MY IEP ACTION PLAN, DATE: December 1998

The target from my Statement of Special Educational Needs or Annual Review I am focusing on is: (if this is relevant) 1) To extend my concentration and attention span; to remain in class. 2) To learn the boundaries of acceptable behaviour, including developing strategies for regulating my need for adult attention. 3) To take more personal responsibility.	

My target(s):   <u>S M A R T</u>

1) To ignore hurtful name calling, so that I stay in class.	What am I like now? 0------------------5--*-------------10 What do I want to achieve? 0------------------5----------*------10
2) To accept the decisions of the teacher so that I stay in class.	What am I like now? 0------------------5*----------------10 What do I want to achieve? 0------------------5-----*----------10
3) To stay out of other boys' business so that I stay out of trouble.	What am I like now? 0----------------*--5---------------10 What do I want to achieve? 0------------------5-----*----------10

<u>What will I do in order to achieve my target?</u>
1) I will try to ignore hurtful comments, if they get too much for me I shall tell the teacher, so that they can deal with it.

2) I will try to listen carefully to everything the teacher has to say and accept this without walking out of class.

3) I will try to concentrate on my own task in class.

<u>Evaluation</u>

I have been working on my targets for ...6... weeks.

Percentage achieved.........75... I feel I   *need*   don't need   more time on target 1.

Percentage achieved.........90... I feel I   need   ***don't need***   more time on target 2.

Percentage achieved.........70... I feel I   *need*   don't need   more time on target 3.

Signed ....(pupil and staff member)   Date...............

MY IEP ACTION PLAN, DATE: February 1999

The target from my Statement of Special Educational Needs or Annual Review I am focusing on is: (if this is relevant)

1) To think before I act so that when I am upset or angry a physical confrontation does not follow.

2) To develop social interactive skills and learn more positive ways of relating to adults and peers.

3) To develop self-confidence and self-esteem.

My target(s):   <u>S M A R T</u>

My target(s)	Scale
1) To ignore hurtful name calling, so that I keep myself to myself.	<u>What am I like now?</u> 0------------------5----*------------10 <u>What do I want to achieve?</u> 0------------------5----------*------10
2) To stay out of other boys' business so that I stay out of trouble.	<u>What am I like now?</u> 0------------------5----*------------10 <u>What do I want to achieve?</u> 0------------------5----------*-----10
3) To be invited to stay in school in the evening for activities and to sleep the night.	<u>What am I like now?</u> 0*------------------5----------------10 <u>What do I want to achieve?</u> 0------------------5------------*----10

<u>What will I do in order to achieve my target?</u>
1) I will try to ignore hurtful comments, if they get too much for me I shall tell the teacher, so that they can deal with it.

2) I will try to concentrate on my own task in class, keeping busy with my own work.

3) I will try to have days in school without any major upsets.

<u>Evaluation</u>

I have been working on my targets for ...6... weeks.

Percentage achieved.........65... I feel I   <u>***need***</u>   don't need   more time on target 1.

Percentage achieved.........80... I feel I   <u>***need***</u>   don't need   more time on target 2.

Percentage achieved.........50... I feel I   <u>***need***</u>   don't need   more time on target 3.

Signed ....(pupil and staff member)   Date..............

<u>MY IEP ACTION PLAN, DATE:</u> April 1999

The target from my Statement of Special Educational Needs or Annual Review I am focusing on is: (if this is relevant) 1) To think before I act so that when I am upset or angry a physical confrontation does not follow. 2) To develop social interactive skills and learn more positive ways of relating to adults and peers. 3) To develop self-confidence and self-esteem.	

My target(s):   <u>S M A R T</u>

1) To ignore hurtful name calling, so that I keep myself to myself.	<u>What am I like now?</u> 0------------------5--*--------------10 <u>What do I want to achieve?</u> 0------------------5------------*----10
2) To stay out of other boys' business so that I stay out of trouble.	<u>What am I like now?</u> 0------------------5----------*-------10 <u>What do I want to achieve?</u> 0------------------5-------------*--10
3) To be invited to stay in school in the evening for activities and to sleep the night.	<u>What am I like now?</u> 0------------------5*----------------10 <u>What do I want to achieve?</u> 0------------------5----------*------10

<u>What will I do in order to achieve my target?</u>   1) I will try to ignore hurtful comments, if they get too much for me I shall tell the teacher, so that they can deal with it.
2) I will try to concentrate on my own task in class, keeping busy with my own work.
3) I will try to have days in school without any major upsets.

<u>Evaluation</u>   I have been working on my targets for ...6... weeks.

Percentage achieved.........80... I feel I   need   ***don't need***   more time on target 1.

Percentage achieved.........65... I feel I   ***need***   don't need   more time on target 2.

Percentage achieved.........70... I feel I   ***need***   don't need   more time on target 3.

Signed ....(pupil and staff member)   Date...............

The Edith Borthwick School

TOTAL COMMUNICATION POLICY
and STATEMENTS of INTENT

'To work with me
You have to listen to me
And you can't just listen with your ears
Because it will go to your head too fast
You have to listen with your whole body
If you listen slow
Some of what I say
Will enter your heart'

Canadian student with
additional learning needs

'It is vitally important to realise that somebody with even the most profound
learning difficulty will be able to communicate spontaneously, to some degree,
through one of the Natural Modalities (speech, writing/reading, gesture, body
language, facial expression, touch, vocalisation)'

ENABLE

INTRODUCTION

This policy has been developed by a group of professionals from education
and health services working with pupils and students at The Edith Borthwick
School. Advice and information has been gathered from a number of sources
which are acknowledged as appropriate. The policy represents a shared
understanding of, and commitment to, the principles of total
communication as a basic human right. This policy communicates these
principles and associated actions to all staff involved with pupils and students
at The Edith Borthwick School.

DEFINITION

Total Communication is understood to mean the way in which people make their needs, desires, personal preferences and feelings known to other people through:

- speech
- reading, writing, using symbols
- gesture and signing
- facial expressions
- body language
- touch
- vocalisation

and through the use of:

- listening skills
- social skills, including mirroring, turn-taking
- intensive interaction
- response and understanding
- touching and leading
- visual and written prompts
- objects of reference, sensory and tactile prompts
- eye contact and other modes of physical and facial expression
- signing systems (e.g. Makaton)
- symbol systems (e.g. Writing with Symbols)
- social use of language
- IT
- alternative and augmentative communication (electronic communication aids, communication aids)
- visual 'passports'

PRINCIPLES

Total communication is based on the principles of:

- Equal opportunities for all pupils and students
- Pupil/student rights to full access to all aspects of the school curriculum
- Rights to express views, choices, needs, wants and feelings
- Rights to be understood
- Entitlement to be approached at an appropriate level to meet needs at all times
- Entitlement to access the full range of communication modes outlined above
- Encouraging motivation to increased and enhanced communication for all

The Edith Borthwick School fully endorses the ASHA Communication Bill of Rights (1992).

WHO IS TOTAL COMMUNICATION FOR?

- Pupils who have communication difficulties
- Pupils who wish to communicate better with those who have communication difficulties
- Staff (teachers, professionals from health [speech and language therapists, physiotherapists and occupational therapists in particular], social services and other agencies, learning support assistants, mid-day assistants, administrative staff, technicians, catering staff, volunteers, cleaning and caretaking staff, escorts) in order to facilitate the highest possible access to communication
- Parents/carers and family members who wish to understand, and communicate better with, those who have communication difficulties

STATEMENT OF INTENT

We intend to empower pupils and students through communication in order to give them increased self-esteem, confidence, competence, independence, ability to make and sustain relationships and participation in informed decision-making leading to more control over their own lives.

To achieve this we intend to develop all the strands of total communication described above and organise them into a 'common language' in order to select the most appropriate modes of communication to meet individual needs. In order to do this we will need to:

- continue to offer and deliver Makaton courses, differentiated and targeted at professionals, parents/carers, children and young people;
- continue to raise the expectations of staff, pupils/students, parents/carers through:
    - examing teaching strategies;
    - providing INSET – demonstration, pairing, etc;
    - providing opportunities for students to join classes to learn signing;
    - encouraging students as teachers;
    - reviewing communication through the PSHE curriculum;
    - examining the further use of accredited courses;
    - organising exchanges of teaching and learning support staff within the school to experience ranges of needs;
    - producing an explicit open house policy for teachers', LSAs' and students' learning;
- accepting the responsibility to practice total communication – particularly through assemblies and other whole school events and activities, and through awareness and communication of IEP targets;
- differentiating for individual and group work, adapting the way we communicate according to individual needs (with reference to personal targets, ranges of teaching and learning strategies);
- emphasising the use of sign and symbol alongside verbal and written communication;
- producing a total communication handbook and resources;
- developing communication passports for a range of pupils/students;
- investigating a project to increase the use of total communication in the wider community (link schools/college/work providers/voluntary sector, etc);
- putting in place a procedure for accessing equipment and advice from ACE, Wolfson Centre, Meldreth Manor, etc;
- considering the purchase of consultancy from ACE;
- producing an action plan, costed and with clear tasks and responsible people to carry out the above work.

We would like to thank the following working group members for their contribution to the formulation of this document: Chris Gamble, Margaret Olsen, Jenny Walker, Frances Houseago, Chris Carruth, Linda Raffray, Kay Shaw, Susan Carpenter, Cathi Howell, Beccy Frances, Mike Jelly.

Ratified by Curriculum Committee on 13.9.99

Appendix 8

From *Top Ten Thinking Tactics* (see 'Resources' section), with acknowledgements to Mike Lake, Marjorie Needham, and Questions Publishing.

ACTIVITY ONE– GETTING THE RIGHT ORDER

Suggested Lesson-Plan:

Task 1

Give out Sheet (1). Get the class to discuss what the pictures show in Sequence A and in what order they are. Does the given order make sense? The class need to agree that the numbers 1, 2, 3 in the small boxes refer to a "correct sequence". Discuss why that suggested sequence is correct.

Ask the class to inspect Sequence B. Discuss the meaning and purpose of these four pictures. What is the task? As a class, they could come to an agreement as to the best order, and each child could be asked to fill in order 1, 2, 3, 4 in the blank boxes. Or, if you prefer, the children could solve this one individually or in pairs. Suggested order is 2, 4, 1, 3.

Task 2

When all are clear about the nature and purpose of Sheet (1), hand out Sheet (2). Let the children (either individually or in pairs) solve the two sequences and fill in the boxes to show the order. Suggested order for Sequence C is 4, 1, 3, 2. For Sequence D, the suggested order is 1, 3, 2, 4.

Either during the solving process or afterwards, encourage discussion of the contents of the two Sequences. For example, the children could be encouraged to discuss sequences which span centuries of customs, habits, dress, living conditions, etc.

Eating habits and preferences can be discussed. Why are meals different at different times of day? Is it just convention? Is it meant to aim at balance? Do you build up different needs or expectation about food at different times of day? Sequence D should suggest several lines of discussion concerning customs changing over time, particulary in regard to male and female roles.

Mediation:

Remember, mediation is only a process of helping children to become active and effective learners – which all good teachers have in mind, knowing the stages of development of their pupils.

Questioning, waiting, repeating, prompting and modelling all take time, of course. It's far quicker and easier to **give** an answer. In fact, with today's demands on time, it's often necessary to do so. To get the best out of this programme, however, we would suggest that (within reason) you aim at a mediating rather than an instructional approach.

Because your central aim is to promote habits of active, purposeful, confident learning, two good rules of thumb are:

1. **DON'T TELL A CHILD WHY S/HE IS WRONG**; try to elicit a changed response through QUESTIONS (guiding as little or as much as necessary).

2. **DO TELL A CHILD WHY S/HE IS RIGHT** – to encourage feelings of confidence based on reality, not on guesswork.

Transfer:

What other situations can the children think of where at first everything seemed too confusing to understand – yet where it all became much easier once they had decided what the problem really was? For example, a page of maths where you can't properly read the instructions; a new project where you've missed some of the instructions; a quarrel in the playground whose cause and results are confusing.

My name is _____

The tactics I am using are _____

_____

Activity One – Getting the Right Order (1)

A

 3

 1

 2

B

My name is_____

The tactics I am using are _____

_____

Activity One – Getting the Right Order (2)

C

D

Appendix 9

From *Top Ten Thinking Tactics* (see 'Resources' section), with acknowledgements to Mike Lake, Marjorie Needham, and Questions Publishing.

ACTIVITY FIVE- A TIME AND A PLACE

Suggested Lesson-Plan:

Task 1
Hand out the sheets. Encourage scanning and discussion of the whole page. Is there any connection between Sequence A and Picture B? Suggest concentrating on Sequence A first. What is the task? (A sequencing one.)

Get the children to write in their solutions – either on their own or in pairs. Suggested order is 5, 1, 4, 3, 2.

Initiate a class discussion of the time sequence involved and how it necessitates changes of **place** as well, e.g. you wouldn't knead dough in a field.

Discuss how some children **changed** their plan when their first hypothesis didn't seem to work out.

Task 2
For picture B, "After you", read out the instructions (and repeat them as needed) once the class has agreed on the main theme of the picture.

Instructions: "The picture shows a sinking boat on a stormy sea. There are several people and a dog on board, all numbered. The rescue helicopter can only take **one** person or animal off at a time. Even if it's a small child, only one person at a time can fit into the harness. Which person would you rescue first? Which second, and so on? Put the number of the person you would rescue first in the first box. Put the number of your second choice in the second box, and so on, until you've filled in all twelve. Remember, the boat could go down at any moment."

The children could work individually or in pairs on this task, which should be expected to involve several changes of mind and rubbings out as **rules** begin to present themselves. For example, a child might initially decide that the toddler should be saved first; then the person who might be the mother, to look after him; then the old man, because he seems helpless . . . and then suddenly realise that s/he is mixing the very young and the very old. Should **all** the young go first? Or

should the reverse hold? (These would constitute rules.) Or rather, should the order be based on degree of helplessness – and the original order be kept? (This would constitute another, perhaps conflicting, perhaps overriding rule.) What about captain? Should he go last? Or first? Is he most important? Where is he most important?

Of course, there are no right and wrong answers. Each child needs to be able to argue why s/he has eventually settled on the chosen order.

In Task 2, time **and** place are involved, because length of time lived is a factor which, to some extent, will determine the children's placing (positioning) in the sequence.

This task obviously lends itself to a discussion, during which the class could be encouraged to debate and perhaps agree upon certain rules.

Remember, there should be no attempt to **make** everyone agree with the rules. The important factors are:

1. Seeing the need for rules to aid behaviour.

2. Being clear about why **you** hold a particular rule.

3. Being able to justify, **clearly**, to other people.

4. Accepting that others may hold different views.

Further Possibilities for Extended Discussion:
Although the children may already have been **led** to consider certain ideas in this exercise, rather than given time to bring up whatever they like, this may be an appropriate point at which to introduce the full version of the "community of enquiry", since they will probably have developed some reasonably strong views while trying to justify their choices in Task 2.

If you found time to encourage discussions along the lines suggested in Activity Three, you will probably not find the "community of enquiry" very different. Nor, for many teachers nowadays, is it all that different from what they are doing much of the time anyway.

My name is _____

The tactics I am using are _____

_____

Activity Five – A Time and a Place

A

<table>
<tr><td></td><td></td><td></td><td></td><td></td></tr>
</table>

My name is _____

The tactics I am using are _____

_____

Activity Five – A Time and a Place

B. "After you"

1. Old Man
2. Young Girl
3. Young Boy
4. Dog
5. Adolescent Boy
6. Young Man
7. Young Woman
8. Toddler
9. Adolescent Girl
10. Middle-aged Man
11. Middle-aged Woman
12. Captain

Emergent Student Data 1994/97

About Me	1994	1997
I keep my thoughts to myself	(11/92%)	(5/42%)
I can't make my mind up	(7/58%)	(4/34%)
I don't feel able to trust other people	(7/58%)	(3/25%)
I get upset very easily	(6/50%)	(3/25%)
I tend to act without thinking of the consequences	(6/50%)	(4/34%)
I am often bored	(7/58%)	(5/42%)
I don't say what I mean	(6/50%)	(3/25%)
I tend to fool around a lot	(5/42%)	(1/8%)
I am often angry	(6/50%)	(5/42%)
I am worried about the future	(7/58%)	(2/16%)
My temper gets me into trouble	(6/50%)	(6/50%)
Other people often get in my way	(6/50%)	(5/42%)
I don't like to have any responsibility	(6/50%)	(1/8%)
Other people don't seem to understand me	(6/50%)	(3/25%)
I don't like the way I look	(4/34%)	(2/16%)
I spend too much time on my own	(5/42%)	(4/34%)
I don't get enough attention from other people	(5/42%)	(3/25%)
Most people don't approve of what I do	(5/42%)	(3/25%)
I am shy and quiet with other people	(4/34%)	(3/25%)

About School	1994	1997
I am afraid of some people in school	(8/65%)	(2/16%)
I make life difficult for teachers	(8/65%)	(3/25%)
I don't like being told what to do	(8/65%)	(5/42%)
I am frequently late in getting into school	(7/58%)	(0/0%)
I often seem to be in trouble at school	(6/50%)	(2/16%)
I don't have any friends at school	(6/50%)	(3/25%)
I sometimes miss lessons	(6/50%)	(4/34%)
I don't pay attention in class	(6/50%)	(4/34%)
I bully other students	(6/50%)	(3/25%)
School work is too easy for me	(5/42%)	(7/58%)
I would rather not be at school	(6/50%)	(5/42%)
I get treated different from other students	(5/42%)	(2/16%)
Some of the damage in school is caused by me	(6/50%)	(1/8%)
School work is too hard for me	(4/34%)	(3/25%)

About My Social Life	1994	1997
I feel quite lonely	(9/75%)	(3/25%)
I spend most of my time at home	(10/83%)	(3/25%)
I don't have enough friends	(10/83%)	(3/25%)
I never seem to keep a friend for long	(10/83%)	(3/25%)
I don't have enough to do outside of school	(8/65%)	(7/58%)
Some of my friends get me into trouble	(8/65%)	(4/34%)
The people I get on with are mostly adults	(8/65%)	(3/25%)
It takes me a long time to make a friend	(8/65%)	(3/25%)
I don't really have a social life	(8/65%)	(4/34%)
I don't have a close friend	(6/50%)	(3/25%)
I don't get on with adults very well	(6/50%)	(3/35%)
Other people seem to copy what I do	(5/42%)	(6/50%)
No one trusts me	(6/50%)	(3/25%)
I enjoy being the centre of attention	(6/50%)	(4/34%)

References

ACE (1995) *Children's Voices in School Matters*. London: ACE.

Ainscow, M. (1999) *Understanding the Development of Inclusive Schools*. London: Falmer Press.

Audit Commission/HMI (Her Majesty's Inspectorate) (1992) *Getting the Act Together*. London: HMSO.

Cohen, L. and Manion, L. (1994) *Research Methods in Education*, 4th edn. London: Routledge.

Covey, S. (1992) *Principle-Centred Leadership*. London: Simon & Schuster.

de Bono, E. (1993) *Teach Your Child How to Think*. Harmondsworth: Penguin.

DES (Department of Education and Science) (1981) *The Education Act 1981*. London: HMSO.

DES (Department of Education and Science) (1989) *Discipline in Schools – Report of the Committee of Enquiry chaired by Lord Elton*. London: HMSO.

DES (Department of Education and Science) (1989) *Personal and Social Education from 5 to 16: Curriculum Matters* 14. London: HMSO.

DES (1990) *Circular Number 8/90 – Records of Achievement*. London: HMSO.

DfE (Department for Education) (1994) *Code of Practice on the Identification and Assessment of Special Educational Needs*. London: HMSO.

DfEE (Department for Education and Employment) (1997) *Excellence for All Children – Meeting Special Education Needs*. London: DfEE.

DfEE (1998) *Meeting Special Educational Needs: A Programme of Action*. London: DfEE.

DfEE/QCA (Qualifications and Curriculum Authority) (1999) *The National Curriculum for England*. London: DfEE/QCA.

Feuerstein, R. *et al.* (1980) *Instrumental Enrichment: An Intervention for Cognitive Modifiability*. Baltimore, Md.: University Park Press.

Fielding, M., Fuller, A. and Loose, T. (1999) 'Taking pupil perspectives seriously: the central place of pupil voice in primary school improvement', in Southworth, G. and Lincoln, P. *Supporting Improving Primary Schools*. London: Falmer Press.

Fullan, M. (1992) *What's Worth Fighting for in Headship?* Buckingham: Open University Press.

Fullan, M. and Hargreaves, A. (1992) *What's Worth Fighting for in Your School?* Buckingham: Open University Press.

Galloway, D., Armstrong, D. and Tomlinson, S. (1994) *The Assessment of Special Educational Needs: Whose Problem?* London: Longman.

Gardner, H. (1993) *Multiple Intelligences: The Theory in Practice.* New York: Basic Books.

Garner, P. (1995) 'Sense or nonsense? Dilemmas in the SEN Code of Practice', *Support for Learning* 10(1), 3–7.

Gersch, I. (1996) 'Listening to Children in Educational Contexts', in Davie, R., Upton, G. and Varma, V. *The Voice of the Child.* London: Falmer Press.

Handy, C. (1995) *The Age of Unreason.* London: Arrow Books.

Handy, C. and Aitken, R. (1986) *Understanding Schools as Organisations.* Harmondsworth: Penguin.

Hart, S. (1996) *Beyond Special Needs – Enhancing Children's Learning Through Innovative Thinking.* London: Paul Chapman Publishing.

Hornby, G. (1995) 'The *Code of Practice*: boon or burden?', *British Journal of Special Educational Needs* 22(3), 116–119.

Kendall, H. (1998) 'The West Berkshire Approach', *Nursing Times* 84(27), 33–4.

Lawrence, D. (1987) *Enhancing Self-esteem in the Classroom.* London: Paul Chapman Publishing.

Lawson, H. (1992) *Practical Record Keeping for Special Schools – Resource Materials for Staff Development.* London: David Fulton Publishers.

McGuinness, C. (1999) 'From thinking skills to thinking classrooms: a review and evaluation of approaches for developing pupils' thinking', in *DfEE Research Report RR115.* London: DfEE.

Mittler, P. (1996) 'Preparing for self-advocacy', in Carpenter, B., Ashdown, R. and Bovair, K. (eds) *Enabling Access – Effective Teaching and Learning for Pupils with Learning Difficulties.* London: David Fulton Publishers.

Mosley, J. (1993) *Turn Your School Around.* Wisbech: Learning Development Aids.

Mosley, J. (1996) *Quality Circle Time in the Primary Classroom.* Wisbech: Learning Development Aids.

Noonan, E. (1990) *Counselling Young People.* London: Routledge.

Ramjhun, A. F. (1995) *Implementing the Code of Practice for Children with Special Educational Needs – A Practical Guide.* London: David Fulton Publishers.

Robson, C. (1993) *Real World Research: A Resource for Social Scientists and Practitioner-researchers.* Oxford: Blackwell.

Rushton, P. and Harwick, J. (1994) 'Pupil participation in their own Records of Achievement', in Rose, R. *et al.* (eds) *Implementing the Whole Curriculum for Pupils with Learning Difficulties.* London: David Fulton Publishers.

Sammons, P., Hillman, J. and Mortimore, P. (1995) *Key Characteristics of Effective Schools.* London: Institute of Education.

Savel, J. M., Twohig, P. T. and Rachford, D. L. (1986) 'Empirical status of Feuerstein's "Instrumental Enrichment" (FIE) technique as a method of teaching thinking skills', *Review of Educational Research* 56, 381–409.

SEAC (School Examination and Assessment Council) (1990) *Records of Achievement in Primary Schools.* London: SEAC.

Sebba, J. and Sachdev, D. (1997) *What Works in Inclusive Education?* Ilford, Essex: Barnardos.

Sharron, H. (1994) *Changing Children's Minds: Feuerstein's Revolution in the Teaching of Intelligence.* London: Souvenir Press.

Skrtic, T. M. (1991) 'Students with special educational needs: artefacts of the traditional curriculum', in Ainscow, M. (ed.) *Effective Schools for All.* London: David Fulton Publishers.

Thiessen, D. (1997) 'Knowing about, acting on behalf of, and working with primary pupils' perspectives: Three levels of engagement with research', in Pollard, A., Thiessen, D. and Filer, A. (eds) *Children and their Curriculum.* London: Falmer Press.

Tilstone, C. (1991) 'Pupils' views', in Tilstone, C. (ed.) *Teaching Pupils with Severe Learning Difficulties.* London: David Fulton Publishers.

Tilstone, C. (1998) 'Recording Evidence', in Tilstone, C. (ed.) *Observing Teaching and Learning – Principles and Practice.* London: David Fulton Publishers.

Tisdall, E. K. M. (1994) 'Why not consider citizenship?: a critique of post-school transitional models for young disabled people', *Disability and Society* 9(1), 3–17.

Tyne, J. (1994) 'Advocacy: not just another subject', in Rose, R. *et al.* (eds) *Implementing the Whole Curriculum for Pupils with Learning Difficulties.* London: David Fulton Publishers.

Wade, B. and Moore, M. (1993) *Experiencing Special Education.* Buckingham: Open University Press.

Index